TRENTYPO —

studies in jazz

Institute of Jazz Studies, Rutgers University
General Editors: *Dan Morgenstern & Edward Berger*

Studies in Jazz No. 10

Metuchen, N.J., & London, 1990 □

The Scarecrow Press and the Institute

Reminiscing in Tempo:

The Life and Times of a Jazz Hustler

TEDDY REIG
with
EDWARD BERGER

of Jazz Studies, Rutgers University

ML
429
.R4A3
1990

British Library Cataloguing-in-Publication data available

Library of Congress Cataloging-in-Publication data

Reig, Teddy
 Reminiscing in tempo : the life and times of a jazz hustler / by Teddy Reig,
with Edward Berger.
     p.   cm.—(Studies in jazz : no. 10)
 Includes bibliographical references and index.
 ISBN 0-8108-2326-8
 1. Reig, Teddy.   2. Sound recording executives and producers—United
States—Biography.   I. Berger, Edward.   II. Title.   III. Series.
 ML429.R4A3   1990
 338.7′6178165149′092—dc20
 [B]   90-36355

CONTENTS

iv **Contents**

EDITOR'S FOREWORD

To INTRODUCE A NEW WORK by my esteemed colleague, friend and co-editor Ed Berger is a very special pleasure—the more so since he, as co-author of *Benny Carter: A Life in American Music*, helped to launch this series. This book documents the life and times of Teddy Reig, literally an outsized character in an environment where characters were hardly in short supply. Theodore Samuel Reig (1918-1984) does not appear in the *New Grove Dictionary of Jazz*, though many who contributed far less to the music do. For purposes of categorization (a practice he abhorred) he was a member of the genus "record producer," later renamed "A & R man," but Teddy was *sui generis*.

I first saw Teddy, who then weighed in at well over 300 pounds, at the Royal Roost around 1947. As fellow habitués of the New York jazz scene, our paths frequently crossed after that—it was impossible not to notice Teddy wherever he might appear—but it wasn't until 1961, on the occasion of the memorable record date that brought together the entire Count Basie and Duke Ellington orchestras, that I got to see Teddy in his element.

He was not in charge at that session, but clearly knew more about what was going down musically than the man in the booth. Later that year, I did see him in action at a date of his own, one of which he was justly proud, the Basie-Benny Carter collaboration, *The Legend*. I had observed enough A & R men at work to find the rapport between him and the musicians extraordinary, and his grasp of the music equally so. Unlike some of his colleagues in the producing game, Teddy couldn't read a score, but he knew how to communicate with the players about what was in those notes. He didn't interfere, but when he was needed, he was there. And he was a master at breaking tension; he knew how to get laughs.

But Teddy Reig, as the reader will learn, was not a jolly fat man. He was tough, and sometimes it didn't take much provocation for him to show that side of his nature. By the time he became a regular at the Institute of Jazz Studies, Teddy had mellowed. Yet he still knew what he wanted and how to get it, and as Ed Berger explains, this book is his last, posthumous, hustle.

Like so many of Teddy's hustles, however, it was not motivated by mere self-interest. Teddy had a story to tell, a story that had relevance beyond his own role in it, and he knew that time was running out. In Ed Berger he found not only a good and knowledgeable listener, but also someone he could trust. Teddy was nothing if not a shrewd judge of character, and he quickly realized that he could speak freely to Ed about the things he had seen and done and rely on Ed's good judgment. And while he had a scheme in mind, he was also genuinely fond of Ed. I can still hear him approaching down the hall, his rough way of opening the door, and his call of "Boiger . . . is Boiger here?" Teddy knew how to make an entrance.

And with this book—his story fleshed out with recollections from people close to him and a record of his professional achievements—Teddy Reig shows that he also knew, good actor that he was, how to make an exit. I miss Teddy, and I know Ed does too.

DAN MORGENSTERN
Director, Institute of Jazz Studies
Rutgers University

INTRODUCTION

THERE ARE FEW NOOKS in the music world of the mid-1940s through the early 1970s that Teddy Reig did not penetrate. Although unknown to the public, he was largely responsible for capturing one of the most influential and enduring bodies of recordings in jazz: Charlie Parker's work on Savoy. Had he done nothing else, this accomplishment alone would have assured his place in history. But he continued to document the development of the new music through his work with a whole range of seminal artists on Savoy, and later, on his own label, Roost. He produced Miles Davis's and Stan Getz's first recordings as leaders. In the mid-1950s, while with Roulette, Teddy became Count Basie's right-hand man, and revealed an uncanny understanding of the Basie orchestra's "chemistry" (as Teddy called it), and how to capture it in a studio. Beyond jazz, Teddy made his presence felt in rhythm and blues and rock and roll through his prescient direction of the careers of Paul Williams and others. He also made his mark in the field of Latin music, recording not only well-known figures, such as Willie Bobo, Machito and Candido, but also seeking out some native Cuban artists. No matter what the music or era, Teddy elicited the best from his artists. His relationship with them went beyond the studio walls, however. He was a friend and confidant of many of the leading figures in American music.

Teddy Reig was the ultimate hustler, and this book is his final hustle. When I first began interviewing Teddy, I had no intention of collaborating on his autobiography. The Institute of Jazz Studies was engaged in an oral history project, and Teddy seemed an ideal subject. In fact, it was Benny Carter who first said, "You have to talk to Teddy Reig!" Shortly after Carter's suggestion, Teddy himself showed up at the Institute, looking for some photos. Though not in the best of health, he was still an impressive figure of imposing size, bearded, with fedora and cane. Within minutes, he was holding court, regaling the Institute staff with tales of 52nd Street and all matter of jazz lore. Discovering a captive, if not willing, audience, he began dropping by often. Early in 1980, I invited Teddy to appear on the Institute's weekly radio show, "Jazz from the Archives," on WBGO-Newark. He was a natural, and reminisced for three hours, with musical interludes devoted to the historic sessions he produced. The show drew some audience response, and in June he returned for another installment. In 1983, Teddy agreed to be interviewed at length for the oral history project. At that time, he first proposed that I assist in preparing his autobiography. He had obviously given it some thought, even to the point of choosing a title: *Reminiscing in Tempo*. I declined, citing other commitments. Actually, I had gotten to know Teddy well enough to realize the pitfalls of working so closely with a character who, despite his considerable charm and charisma, could be unreasonably demanding and volatile. I did assure him, however, that he and another collaborator could use the transcripts of our interviews as the basis for his book. Teddy was not happy, but agreed to proceed, and in July of 1983, we conducted the first of many interview sessions.

I should have recognized his scheme early on, when several mutual acquaintances began to ask me about the book I was doing with Teddy. I demurred, but to no avail. It was not until after Teddy's death on September 29, 1984, that the full implications of his plot surfaced. At the memorial service, it seemed that most of the congregation made a point of telling me how much they were looking forward to "the book"; Teddy had obviously told everyone he knew we were collaborating on this project! Under the circumstances, I could hardly refuse to carry out what was in essence his last wish, even if it was also his last hustle.

Interviewing Teddy was both fascinating and frustrating. I have few illusions about the veracity of everything Teddy told me. He had a natural tendency, as do most people, to inflate his own role at times. On the other hand, he maintained an overall honesty about himself and his character. Consequently, we are spared much of the self-righteousness of other industry figures who have written their memoirs. This is

Teddy's story, and I have tried not to change the perspective from which he retells events. I have occasionally corrected obvious errors of fact, such as dates (for which Teddy had a terrible memory).

Because Teddy died before we could cover all aspects of his life and career, I have had to draw on several sources in addition to our oral history interviews. These sources include the two "Jazz from the Archives" programs on WBGO (February and June 1980); Teddy's remarks at the International Association of Jazz Record Collectors panel discussion of record producers (Rochelle Park, New Jersey, August 20, 1983); and a seminar on Count Basie sponsored by the Institute of Jazz Studies in April of 1983. Still, gaps remain. To provide a more complete picture—and several different perspectives—I have included interviews with ten people who were especially close to Teddy at different stages in his life: musicians Leonard Gaskin (interviewed January 20, 1989), Paul Williams (January 25, 1989) and Johnny Smith (March 15, 1989); producers Bob Porter (February 2, 1989), Jerry Wexler (March 9, 1989), Gus Statiras (March 16, 1989) and Pete Spargo (April 11, 1989); music publishing executives Mike Gould (May 27, 1989) and Phil Kahl (May 30, 1989); and Teddy's daughter, Sandra Lovell (February 8, 1989). It is hoped that their observations will not only more fully document the career of Teddy Reig, but will also shed light on many aspects of the music business as a whole.

As their remarks underscore, Teddy was larger than life, full of contradictions, and given to extremes. In more ways than one, he was a man in the middle, straddling different cultures and even manifesting different personalities. He was a street-smart bully who could be moved to tears by a Ben Webster ballad. He recognized and appreciated genius, yet mastered the base practices often needed to reconcile artistic creation with commercial reality. He was the bridge between musicians who knew nothing of business and businessmen who knew nothing of music. Born Jewish, he was attracted to black music early in life and was eventually ostracized by his family for marrying a black woman. As Dizzy Gillespie states, "Teddy moved his soul to Harlem, and lived it to the end."

Teddy was not always altogether successful in balancing all

of the disparate social, cultural and commercial components of his life. Some black musicians viewed him as just another exploiter, albeit a hip one. (An example is the unflattering portrayal of Teddy by Chuck Berry in his autobiography. Berry inadvertently, but perhaps tellingly, refers to Teddy throughout as "Teddy Roag!") To some whites, on the other hand, he was a "nigger lover."

I never knew Teddy in his prime. By the time I met him, he may have mellowed, but he never really changed. Despite the onset of crippling physical infirmity, the fire still burned and surfaced at times. For example, I witnessed one incident of vintage Teddy Reig, reminiscent of his heyday. Teddy had left his car, which had a prominently displayed handicapped sticker, double-parked on a Newark street. When told to move it by a rather sanctimonious policeman, Teddy began to argue. The officer unhooked his nightstick and slowly approached. Teddy countered by brandishing his cane, and proceeded to tell the cop at the top of his lungs, using highly colorful and original language, what he could do with his stick. They stood and glared at each other for a moment and, to my amazement, the cop turned and walked away. Teddy looked at me, winked, and said, "Let's get something to eat."

Teddy Reig not only had a story to tell; he knew how to tell it. In his last years, Teddy occasionally accepted invitations to participate in various conferences on jazz history. Although distinguished panelists preceded him, they were no match for Teddy, who inevitably stole the show. His endless store of "insider" stories were rendered even more hilarious by a comic's sense of delivery and timing. He could also turn serious, however. Perhaps his most poignant public appearance was the April 1983 Basie panel discussion at Rutgers University. Toward the end of a three-hour session, Teddy made a plea for tolerance and understanding on the part of audiences toward artists. Jazz fans and critics, he reminded us, might not always be aware of extenuating circumstances affecting an artist's performance on a given day. As an illustration, he then dropped the bombshell that his beloved wife Netta had died that very morning.

I hope the portrait which emerges is a fair one which not

only documents the events and achievements, but also conveys something of the unique character of Teddy Reig.

EDWARD BERGER
May 1989

ACKNOWLEDGMENTS

MANY PEOPLE CONTRIBUTED to this work in different ways. First, I would like to thank Bob Porter, who was not only an essential source of information, but also a constant source of encouragement. In addition to many other contributions, Bob allowed me to incorporate into the text portions of his interview with Teddy Reig which appeared in the booklet accompanying *Charlie Parker: The Complete Savoy Studio Sessions*.

I am also most grateful to Teddy's daughter, Sandra Lovell, and her husband, Ellsworth, for their cooperation and hospitality. They not only shared their reminiscences, but also allowed me access to Teddy's record collection, and provided many rare photographs.

Leonard Gaskin, Paul Williams, Johnny Smith, Gus Statiras, and Pete Spargo gave unstintingly of their time, and contributed greatly to my understanding of Teddy Reig and the music business. I am deeply indebted to them for their insight and candor. Others who generously shared their memories include Bernie Brightman, Bill Crow, Juggy Gayle, Dizzy Gillespie, Mike Gould, Jack Hooke, Phil Kahl, Jack Silverstein, Murray Slochover, and Jerry Wexler.

I would like to thank Vincent Pelote, John Clement, George Wilson, and Phil Schaap for their discographical assistance. Chuck Stewart, Mitchell Seidel, Leonard Gaskin, Leonard Feather and William Kane (Teddy's uncle) were kind enough to supply photos.

Ron Welburn was Coordinator of the Jazz Oral History Project at the time of the Reig interviews, and he brought his skill to bear on several of the sessions.

My friend and colleague Dan Morgenstern provided his customary editorial expertise, as did my brother Ken Berger. And, finally, special thanks to Benny Carter for first suggesting the project, and for his continued encouragement.

Teddy Reig (November 23, 1918-September 29, 1984)

PROLOGUE

I'M AT THE AGE where I have a limited number of bars left to play. Few people have had the chance to see the music business from behind the counter of a record shop, to go on the road with the bands, first as a band boy, then as road manager and eventually as a record producer and record company owner. I want the world to know about the many things that go into the music besides the actual performance.

I'm sixty-five years old and never did a day's work. This business is still supporting me. I've been a hustler all my life, up to the point of death, at which time I split. I was torn between love for the musicians and tolerance for the guys with the money. Making records is like being married: you have to give and take. You raise your voice, then you stroke like a pussycat.

I was one of the lucky ones. Those of us in the business were just grateful to have been there, to have heard these geniuses and to have participated in their lives. Those were fantastic days. Today it's a whole new world. Now you play a bad chorus and they say, "It's O.K. Come back tomorrow and mix it in." The only thing we mixed in those days was a malted.

CHAPTER ONE:
BEGINNINGS

I WAS BORN IN Harlem on 110th Street, when it was a white neighborhood. November 23, 1918, was the date. I came from a typical Jewish family: the boy goes to school, when he reaches a certain age they make plans for his marriage, his occupation . . . his life. I rebelled, and then I had no family. For many years, my father sold insurance, and then he became a luggage salesman—now they call it a "manufacturer's representative." My family was still trying to figure out what to do with me when my father bought a candy store. I used to go in there and help, and the plan was for me to finish school and become a pharmacist. I just couldn't see myself standing in a candy store, or as a druggist. I wanted to be a free spirit. I began getting interested in music around sixteen or seventeen when the big band craze hit. When I mentioned the music business, my father almost hit me in the head.

I went to New Utrecht High School, but never got a diploma. I stood up and sang the national anthem, and during the part about the land of the free and the home of the brave, I said, "You forgot to say how brave you've got to be to be free." They wouldn't sign my diploma. The principal was always on top of me for my liberal thoughts. I began my career by leading a lunchroom riot which made headlines in the *New York Times*. We had discovered that the principal was dispersing money for cookies into his own pocket, not to the "general organization." That was the first time people called me a wild man.

I started going to places like the Sonia Ballroom on Bedford Avenue in Brooklyn. A bunch of us would go to the dances. I'd buy a ticket for a dollar, tiptoe over to the fire escape, and open the door for all the rest of the guys. Eventually we got friendly with the local musicians. About that time, I got a little record player. The Edison Company came out with a combination radio, record player and lamp for $24. That was my first phonograph.

I got to hear some of the great black bands like Andy Kirk, and I began to get a hint of where it was all coming from. I was impressed with the Savoy Sultans and got to know Al Cooper. He used to let me earn some money putting out placards. That was around 1935 or 1936 and it was my first step in the business. Another guy who took me under his wing was a drummer named Arthur Herbert. He was a West Indian, very polished and well-mannered, and he became my guide. When he went to work with Pete Brown, I hung around with Pete, who used to work at the Sonia Ballroom. Then he got an opportunity down on 52nd Street, so I started to creep down there. We didn't have any money—we were like parasites, standing near the doors of places like the Hickory House.

Next, I landed a job as a band boy in Boston on the Shribman circuit. Cy Shribman had a bunch of ballrooms. His life was devoted to Mal Hallett, who had all the great white players: Jack Jenney, Pete Mondello, Teddy Grace, Buddy Welcome. Their theme song was "Boston Tea Party." Of course the expression for reefer was "tea," and down by the docks in Boston you could get all that crap you wanted. The band always had a gang of shit in the bus. We had a trunkful. I was in charge of the bag, and became everybody's buddy— blacks and whites. Cy Shribman liked me and told me that if I ever went back to school, he'd make me a manager. I never went back to school, but Cy hooked me up with the Hudson-DeLange orchestra. I got friendly with Jimmy Van Heusen, who wrote a bunch of songs with Eddie DeLange. I was actually there when they were working on "Heaven Can Wait," which later became a number one hit. I'll never forget that scene! Jimmy would sit at the upright facing the wall and Eddie would be looking over his shoulder. Jimmy plays the first strain, and Eddie sings "Heaven can wait . . ." while Jimmy writes it down. When Jimmy comes to the second strain, Eddie suddenly gets an itch in his balls. He starts scratching and sighs, "This is paradise . . . !" Van Heusen writes it down. The next thing I know, war breaks out between them. When Jimmy found out where the line came from, he didn't want to use it.

By 1942, I was in tight with a lot of musicians. Two of my closest friends were Mike Bryan, the guitarist with Benny Goodman, and the tenor saxophonist Georgie Auld. They helped me a great deal in learning about jazz, but my friendship with them also caused me to serve some time. Mike and Georgie got this idea that they would buy $300 worth of reefer for a lady friend. Because she had no idea what anything cost, the plan was that I would go uptown and get $100 worth and then we would split the other two hundred. In those days, for one hundred bucks, you could come back with a real "croakersack." I did it, but as it turned out we were set up. A day or two later they grabbed us and locked us up. This lady had a room in the Hotel Forest, where we used to hang around and listen to records. The papers covered the story and referred to the place as a "reefer parlor."[1] They said the lady was a writer—I don't know what she ever wrote. Her name was Ursula Parrott; it's imprinted on my forehead, I guess. I was sentenced to a year and a day, and it was reduced to nine months and eighteen days.

I did my time at Lexington, Kentucky, which was more like a country club than a jail. Everybody tried to get assigned there by saying, "Oh yeah, I smoke reefer—I'm a drug addict!" It was run like a hospital. Apart from the black-white separation, the Texas bunch had their area, the New York bunch had our area. This one guy I met—Louis Lepke — he had the whole jail paid off. After he found out I was a Jewish kid, I used to get cartons of cigarettes, razor blades, shaving cream, toothpaste, all compliments of Mr. Lepke. A few years later, when Wild Bill Davison was working the Onyx Club, we got friendly with the man who worked the register; anybody who was near the money was our man. This guy turned out to be Lepke's son. About three or four years ago, I ran into Wild Bill, and we got to talking about the Onyx and he remembered the man at the register. He said, "I didn't know his name but I knew he was connected, 'cause when Lepke got the electric chair, he took that week off!"

CHAPTER TWO:
52ND STREET—THE MAKING OF A HUSTLER

AFTER PRISON, MY RELATIONS with my family became even more strained. I went to my father to ask for some money to start a record label and he said, "Records? Are you crazy? You sell aspirins, something people *need* every day!" I was a bad boy—out on the streets every night, and I wasn't in the best of shape when I got home. They'd try to wake me to go to work in the candy store and I'd say, "Forget it."

I naturally gravitated to 52nd Street. Between 6th and 7th Avenues there were three clubs in the early days. Those on the other side of 6th Avenue came later. Most of these places had been speakeasies during Prohibition. When Prohibition ended in 1933, they became little bars and then nightclubs. There was one famous speakeasy: the first brownstone going toward 5th Avenue on the left-hand side. It didn't have a sign or anything. It was for the elite; Mabel Mercer held forth there (this was before Bobby Short came along). None of us went near the place. There was also the Famous Door with Louis Prima and Martha Raye. The blacks were limited to intermission piano players. Then there was the Yacht Club which opened with Fats Waller.

About this time, I started my first little hustle. All of us had to find a way to make a quarter without working, of course. We knew all the guys in the packing rooms at the music publishers—the Strand Building and the Brill Building. We'd give the guy a buck and he'd slip us $10 worth of stocks. Then we'd go back to Brooklyn and sell them to all those bands that played weddings, bar mitzvahs and even funerals.

I began to have a little money in my pocket and started visiting a place called Harry's Bar, which was the first musicians' hangout on 52nd Street. It was six or seven doors below 6th Avenue going west. They served a drink called Silvermet gin. For 15 cents you got a two-ounce shot with Coca-Cola.

4

When you bought three, the house bought you one. So for $2, you could buy a bunch of drinks for a lot of guys, and you'd already be pretty crocked when those free ones started showing up! I'll never forget Silvermet. The classier hangout was the Taft. They would sell you an imported Scotch for 35 cents, plus 6 cents for ginger ale or Coke. Harry's was more popular. Much later there was an incident at the Taft. I went there with Perry Como, who was working in the area with Ted Weems, and with a bunch of Ohio musicians who were working in the studios. Cozy Cole was with us and they wouldn't serve him. Como almost went over the bar to get at the guy who refused to serve Cozy.

We jazz freaks would find all kinds of ways to support our habit. During the week, we'd raid the Salvation Army for records. Then we'd go up to Milt Gabler at the Commodore Music Shop and the Hot Record Society on 7th Avenue and sell them for a quarter or half-dollar each. We had another nice hustle going in the early 1940s. We would buy up all the worn-out records from the jukeboxes at 9 cents a piece. Then we'd take a rag with black shoe polish, shine them up and sell them for a quarter. When we got through, they looked brand new. But when you played them, it sounded like Gravel Gertie singing in Arabic.

That's how we could afford to hang out in the clubs. At Kelly's Stable, where I heard Coleman Hawkins after he returned from Europe, a bottle of beer was 40 cents. They had a bartender named Harry who would try to grab away your bottle. You had to hold it with both hands. If you let go for a second, Harry would snatch it and say, "Alright, what're you havin'?" And if you didn't order something, they'd throw you out.

It was in Kelly's Stable that I got my first real work as a promoter. This was around 1941 or 1942 and Monte Kay, Pete Kameron, Jerry White and I started running jam sessions on Sunday afternoons. We would go uptown to Minton's on Sunday night—that was when all the cats were out—and line up the guys for next week. Monday morning we'd get postcards printed up and send them off. At one of our sessions we had both Ben Webster and Coleman Hawkins. Ben had just come back from California with Duke and was pretty hot with

Theodore S. Reig
912 - 43rd St
Bklyn L. Y.

George Hoeffer Jr
2 East Banks St
Chicago, Illinois

Would appreciate a listing in your
collectors catalog. My main interests are
Louis Armstrong, Piano Solos, Duke
Ellington. Have plenty of Trading material
would like to exchange correspondence
Sincerely
Theodore S. Reig

A 1940 letter to George Hoefer of *Down Beat*

"Just a-Sittin'" and "Cottontail." He told me, "I want Hawk!"
I said, "Okay, we'll get you Hawk." I begged Hawkins to do it
and he agreed, but for $20 which was double what we usually
paid. Sunday came, and Ben went up to the mike, all big, bad
and bold. He growled out a chorus and Hawk egged him on,
saying "C'mon, take some more." Ben looked at him a little
suspiciously but went ahead. And then Hawk took over where
he left off and buried him. When we looked around, there was
no more Ben Webster. He didn't even finish the set, never
mind the gig. That night, we were back at Minton's, lining up
the acts for next week, when in walks Ben, completely crocked.
He's waving a clarinet in his hand, yelling, "Get me Barney
Bigard!"

Minton's was becoming the place to be. It had begun to
attract an audience from downtown—people who heard
about what was happening up there. And then, like all the jazz
joints, you had the pimps waiting for their whores to finish
work and bring them enough money to pay their bills. There
were also the guys like me—on the fringe, trying to get a little
of the meat to eat.

After I served my time for the frame-up, I had to watch my
step because of the probation period. I hung around the candy
store, but by 1943 and 1944 I drifted back to the Street. I
would steal a few bucks from the register, and go out and have
a good time. The first time I took my future wife on a date I
had eight or nine bucks—all in nickels and dimes!

When the war came, I was at a peculiar age—my mid-
twenties. They didn't know whether to take me or not. I
started out 1-A, so when I tried to find a job, no one would
take me because I might get drafted a week later. I finally got a
chance to work at WNEW with Art Ford. Before the interview, I got a lead pipe, wrapped it in some newspaper and went
down to the draft board. The board was made up of a rabbi, a
priest, a politician and the neighborhood wise guy. I walked in
and started banging on the table with the pipe and yelling,
"You cocksuckers are gonna tell me one way or the other!
You're not going to have me on a string like a yo-yo." They
immediately changed me to 4-F. So I was able to go to work
for Art Ford, running around getting records for him. My

girlfriend was really proud of me; I was finally working somewhere.

I still had plenty of time for hustles, though. In those days, record stores had to have a franchise arrangement. In order to sell Victor jazz records, for example, you had to buy X amount of classical records, X amount of needles, even a certain number of empty storage albums. I managed to set up a middleman operation. I would arrange a trade-off between the black and white record stores, so that each would end up with the stuff they could sell. And for my services, I got 10 cents a record.

Another thing I got involved in was an after-hours joint called the Two O'Clock Club. It was in the same building where Birdland was located years later. We opened up around 2 a.m. and had a bunch of lockers where musicians could keep their instruments or whiskey or whatever. Everyone had their own key, and they could buy breakfast and set-ups. Among the members were Pete Brown, the Clarence Profit Trio, Sanford Gold, and Frenchie Coette.

BLACK AND WHITE ON THE STREET

I was always aware of the racial problems of the musicians who were my friends, but around this time it really started to hit home. Through my friend from Brooklyn, bassist Leonard Gaskin, I met Netta, who was to become my wife; she was black.

People always wanted to have someone to look down upon. Blacks would have trouble in dumps on 47th Street, but they could go into the Waldorf Astoria during the worst days of discrimination and there'd be no problem. Most of the bullshit came from the poor people. The education of Mississippi whites was so inferior that they would keep the blacks from getting *any* education, just so they could have someone beneath them.

Going out on the road with a black band was a nightmare. You'd have to figure out exactly where you would eat and sleep. You knew that in one town a Mrs. Johnson had four rooms, someone else had three, and you still had to figure out where to get the laundry done. We would play a dance for a guy and many times we hadn't eaten yet. So the guy would say, "I'll take care of you." He'd send us to a restaurant and they'd take all the prices down and charge us three times as much. And then the pièce de résistance: the promoter would let people in for half a buck apiece to watch us eat!

In the 1950s, I was in Mississippi managing Paul Williams' band the day they signed the civil rights law. I was scared to come out of the hotel. I wouldn't go to the date—I didn't care if they had eighty thousand bucks in the cashbox. I took a cab and waited at a gas station eight miles out of town until the band came in the bus to get me on the way out.

The only time we had trouble on 52nd Street was during the war years. The soldiers and sailors would come from everywhere, and they weren't prepared for the liberal look of the Street. Three soldiers would come in and see a white woman with a black guy and a fight would break out. The Savoy Ballroom was even closed once during the war because of incidents. The only problems came from the crackers.

One incident almost got me sent back to jail. The cops that worked around 52nd Street had a bar where they got free food and drinks. The cops that went on at midnight were really crocked by 4 a.m. One of these guys was standing in the shadows one night and when I walked by he called me a "nigger lover." I said, "Why don't you come into the light and say that?" He did, and I knocked him cold, took his club away from him, and dared him to make a move (I was pretty big in those days, and knew how to use all of it!). I got arrested, and everybody from the Street came to court. I got some help from an acquaintance who was heavy with the law. He managed to make a deal with the judge, and the whole thing was thrown out.

A white man couldn't see a black woman without someone getting the wrong idea. I used to visit my future wife in the building where she lived, on Lefferts Avenue in Brooklyn. The landlady accused her of turning tricks and put her out. We didn't get married until 1948; I could hardly support myself at the time. God knows where I would have been without her.

The real obstacles for black musicians were in the studios, because that's where the steady money was. Later on, when I had some clout, I got into it a few times at the union. They had a rule that if you made an audition for a radio show and the show was bought, then everyone who had done the rehearsal got the job. When they had the first of the Chesterfield shows, Paul Baron had a band that included Red Norvo, Charlie Shavers, Specs Powell, Al Hall and Roy Eldridge. After the audition, an eager beaver bass player named Sid Weiss suddenly replaced Hall. I kept going to Mr. Rosenberg at the union and got nowhere. So I waited until he was running for office, and went down there and broke up the union meeting by screaming at him, "What about the Chesterfield show?" They came after me and I coldcocked the sergeant-at-arms. Eventually they gave the blacks back the jobs.

We were always trying to give our friends a shot to break down the barriers. A couple of times I guess I got carried away. Once, I ended up recording John Simmons and Cozy Cole with a harmonica group. The date called for tympani, which Cozy wasn't too crazy about. Another time, I got him involved in some Irish shit. I didn't give a damn—it was money. The final straw came when they asked me, "Can your man play marimba?" I said, "Motherfucker'll play anything!" When Cozy got to the studio, he took one look at the parts and pulled me aside. "I want to thank you for trying so hard for me," he said, "but next time please ask, or we'll both go down!"

CHAPTER THREE:
STOMPING AT SAVOY

BY 1945, I HAD MIGRATED FROM Harry's Bar to the White Rose, which was where I met my wife. Drinks in the clubs had gone up to 60 cents for a beer and 75 cents for whiskey; who the hell had that? So we'd sit in the White Rose and wait for the cats to come off their sets.

After a while, this little mental patient by the name of Herman Lubinsky started coming around. Herman owned Savoy Records and he would take up a table, spread out all his contracts, and use it like an office. He wouldn't buy a glass of water and never tipped anybody. Then he tried the same thing in the clubs. One night I was sitting on a car bumper in front of the Three Deuces, surveying the scene, and suddenly here

comes Herman flying through the air. "Get the fuck out and
stay out!" they were yelling. "This is a club, not an office." So I
walked up to him and said, "Schmuck, come here. What are
you trying to do with these people?" He said, "I'm trying to
record them." I said, "Listen, I'll make a deal with you. Give
me $100 for four weeks. If I don't double it, I'll give you your
money back." He said, "Alright, come over to Newark tomorrow and we'll talk about it." And that's how I went to work for
Herman Lubinsky.

You have to know what 58 Market Street in Newark, New
Jersey, was all about. At first, Herman sold records only out of
the store, where he had his radio and electronic business. The
record dates were for union scale, which was $60, and the four
guys were each $30. So for $180 you had four sides. If he
could sell 500 from the store, he was in good shape. Then we
got into national distribution and a lot of things began to
happen. Two thousand was like a national hit. We would get a
dollar a record. The whole cost, including the quartet or
quintet, mastering, processing and pressing was about 30 or
35 cents. I'm including royalties which were never paid. I
never heard of Herman paying a royalty!

Herman used to have a good thing going with the copy-
rights of the tunes he recorded. He loved to record originals
which he could copyright. When you owned the copyright you
could control the rate, which was an important thing to these
little record companies. If he owned the tune, he could pay
only a penny, instead of the copyright standard of 2 cents. I
had all I could do once to keep Denzil Best from going after
Herman with a piece of iron in the White Rose over a tune of
Denzil's called "Dee Dee's Dance." "I don't mind giving you
the tune," Denzil argued, "but you're going to hump me in the
payments *and* in the rate!"

Herman also used to try to save money by using a cheap
studio whenever he could get away with it. He used to like to
use Schirmer's which, believe it or not, had a one-armed
engineer. As someone pointed out, it wasn't too bad because
we were recording in mono! This same engineer had a medical
condition which required him to drink wine for his blood. So,
there I was, surrounded by musicians with habits, working
with a drunken engineer with one arm. And today I have to

listen to people tell me that we didn't have enough drums, or that the piano wasn't loud enough! We used to sit with our fingers crossed and pray that, under those circumstances, we could get three minutes of usable music!

Before I was actually employed by Lubinsky at Savoy, I was already going over there for sessions that my friends were doing. My first insight into how Herman operated was the Ben Webster date with Cozy Cole's All Stars.[2] In Ben you had one of the true individuals, and his playing reflected his personality. In "Cottontail" he sounds like four lions getting loose for the first time in a year. Then he could turn around and melt your heart with a ballad. He was outspoken, honest, and he hated Lubinsky! Ben arrived two hours and twenty minutes late for the date, used up ten more minutes arguing with Herman, and then went in and cut four tunes in thirty-five minutes.

My first date as a producer actually came a little before my association with Herman. I got involved with Continental[3] and a guy named Lou Linden who went for a walk and never came back. He was down in Baltimore, and used to send us money to record up here. We did eight sides with Charlie Parker, Dizzy, Don Byas, Clyde Hart, Al Hall, and Specs Powell. Trummy Young sang on four and the others had Rubberlegs Williams. That was the beginning of my making records and it was quite a session. Bird had been subbing the night before with Cootie Williams at the Savoy. Of course at the Savoy you worked until three or four o'clock in the morning, and the recording date was all day Saturday so Bird didn't get much sleep. We got coffee for everyone, and after a few minutes Bird comes up to me and says, "Man, I'm pretty beat. You got a benny?" I didn't, but suggested we get an inhaler. So we did—Bird was a genius at breaking them open and getting the strips out. He threw it into one of the coffee containers, which he thought was his. We found out a week later that it actually was Rubberlegs Williams, who had never taken pills, who got the benny. And that recording is testimony as to what a blues singer on Benzedrine will sound like!

In many ways the Savoy Records job was a dream come true for me. It was just hangin' out, having fun, and getting paid for it, although very weakly with Herman! If I hadn't padded the expense account, I'd have starved. There was talent all over the place and everyone was anxious to earn an extra dollar recording. All the joints on 52nd Street had a capacity of 75 or 100 people, and if the fire department came in on a Saturday night, they'd have been closed down. On 52nd Street there were about seven clubs right next door to one another. They were all basements of brownstones. That's where all the guys hung out, where they got jobs, and where they made reputations. One guy would invite another to play a set on his job. The boss would hear him and give him the off-night, then a full week, and that way he grew.

CUTTIN' TIME

The best music never made it onto record, but was played at cutting contests. Today, to make it big, a guy makes a record, the company hypes it and gives the deejays some freebies, and suddenly he's winning the polls. In the old days to establish yourself, you got your axe out and looked for people to chop up. If you went on the road, you'd get to a new town and there'd be someone who was supposed to be red hot. You'd go to the joint after the dance and cut the guy to ribbons. He'd bleed a little and you'd leave town.

I made friends with Clyde Hart, a musician's musician. Much of my knowledge and love for the music comes from him. Clyde was always at the center of those cutting contests. He was the guy everyone like Roy Eldridge and Don Byas would take with them; he knew all the tunes and could play them in any key and at any tempo. With Clyde, you didn't have to just call "Honeysuckle Rose." He could also play in the unusual keys that were used to trip up the opposition—what we used to call "oriental" keys.

Don Byas was one of the kings of the Street and a rough man at any cutting session. Coleman Hawkins once had a group with Don. They were booked for four weeks, but Hawk broke up the group before that. He told me, "Teddy, there's no need for a man my age to work as hard as this fool from Oklahoma wants me to!" I used to hang out with Don when he went around town looking for people to jam with. One night there was a young man who was making a lot of noise. He was carried away by it all; he had the Lester Young stance, he played "Cherokee" real bright and he thought he was swingin'. He looked over at Don and said, "You want to play something man?" So Don says, "Okay, you call the tune." So he called "Cherokee." When Don got to the 16th bar of the 64-bar chorus, this young man was at the bar in the back of the room ordering doubles; he didn't come back till the last 8 because he was shaking like a leaf. That was the day before one of my dates with Don, and that's why we did "Cherokee."

I had a hand in one famous Don Byas record that I wasn't supposed to be involved in. I was doing a date for Savoy and across the hall Sam Goody was recording Don. I popped in while they were doing "Laura."[4] Don had had a little too much to drink and nobody could handle him. Every time they came near the end, he launched into one of his fabulous cadenzas and kept going well over the three-minute limit. This went on for several takes. Finally, I stood behind Don, and slowly tiptoed over to him and gently took the horn out of his mouth just as the clock read 2:59. Everybody applauded, and Goody

came up and growled, "What do I owe you for this?" I answered, "Give me whatever you want, and let me go down and steal a few records for the rest of your life." He said we had a deal and gave me $10. Sure enough, he let me go to the store and take whatever I wanted right up until he sold the company.

Don Byas *(Courtesy of the Institute of Jazz Studies)*

CHAPTER FOUR:
CAPTURING GENIUS

THE FIRST TIME I HEARD Bird was on "Hootie Blues" with Jay McShann, which was a popular jukebox record. Everybody kept listening to the saxophone solo and didn't know what the hell it was. Later, when Charlie came to New York, Ben Webster came running around spreading the message of Bird. He got Dizzy out of bed and made all of us go up to Monroe's to hear Bird. The after-hours Harlem joints were the only places he could work without a union card. The guy from the union wouldn't go in there, not if he knew what he was doing. When I first spoke with Bird, it was like the first time I met Coleman Hawkins or Benny Carter; these were people I idolized. I was immediately surprised by the way he spoke; he was very proper and articulate.

So many lies have been written about Bird. He was one of the most sensitive, intelligent, tender, loving people I've ever known. Just as an example of what he was about: when Dizzy opened with his big band at the Strand Theater, Bird woke me up and made me get some money because he was broke. I had to find out what he wanted it for because he was doing some things that weren't exactly healthy. So I went with him. We ended up at a florist, where he bought a big bouquet of roses. Like two faggots, we marched down the street and into the backstage of the Strand and he presented them to Dizzy as he came off the bandstand.

Bird's playing says it all. Listen to anybody: Ben, Hawk, Lester, and you'll hear the personality of the artist come through. Bird always had a story to tell—and it was a beautiful story. Sometimes I take some of Bird's up-tempo things and play them at the slower speeds. You can hear the beautiful melody line clearly. It's not just a gang of notes like some of the guys who think they're playing like Bird spew out.

THE KOKO SESSION: RECORDING A CLASSIC[5]

Much to my regret, Tiny Grimes grabbed Bird for four sides for Savoy in 1944. Actually, I was happy because it made me look that much smarter to Herman. I was able to do Bird's first date as a leader, and all the rest of his Savoy sessions. At the record dates Parker was in complete control. In a sense he made it easier for me because I could concentrate on other things. It would have been idiotic for me to suggest anything to Bird, since he was so well organized in his own mind as to who the proper players would be. With someone like Bird, I tried to allow him to display his talents without interference.

Bird was in charge. Always. There was never any question about Bird. Everybody knew what he could do. He played with so much authority! He'd play things and all the guys like John Lewis, Miles, Dizzy, would run to the piano to check the harmonic progressions to determine whether he was crazy or right. And he was always right! He'd turn away and laugh.

On November 26, 1945, the day of "Koko," Bud Powell was supposed to play piano. When I went up to 2040 [7th

Avenue—where many musicians lived] for the "roundup," here comes Bird with Dizzy in tow. I asked, "Where's Bud?" Bird told me Bud went to Philadelphia with his mother to check out a real estate deal. "Dizzy's going to play piano." So we went to the studio and, as usual, everything was going wrong. You have to picture the scene with Herman Lubinsky. He was about five feet four and would sit there with the cigar clamped in his teeth, and all the contracts laid out before him. Before you made a move you had to sign or he wouldn't give you 5 cents. Herman had given Bird a $300 advance on four tunes that he was supposed to write. He only had three and I knew it. I figured we'd get a "head" on the fourth.

From the beginning Charlie's horn was giving him fits; you can hear the squeaks on some of the alternate takes that Herman conveniently saved. Finally it was decided that I would go with Charlie to 48th Street to have the horn fixed—I wasn't going to let him go by himself; he was liable to be gone for a week! While we were gone, the guys in the studio had really partied it up. Miles wasn't worth three dead flies, as Sweets Edison used to say. We still had to do the fourth tune, which was to be "Cherokee," without the melody. I called it "Koko" to keep any idea of "Cherokee" out of Herman's head; I didn't know at the time that he couldn't hear anything but the cash register. But on the first take, they went back into the melody, so I whistled and yelled out "Hold it!" I guess it's my big moment on record, since they issued all the takes from the session.

Because Miles was in no condition to play on "Koko," Dizzy said he would cover on trumpet. This led people to believe that it wasn't him, but Sadik Hakim on piano. This I will contest until my dying day. Sadik was there, and we were going to use him, but he was on transfer from the union. The union man showed up and Sadik did a double boogie and split through the side door. If you listen closely, there is nobody but Dizzy on piano.[6] Dizzy is on trumpet in the opening ensemble with Bird. When Bird gets two or three bars into his solo, you'll hear someone at the piano go "choink, choink." That was Dizzy letting Bird know he had arrived. In order to get him back to the trumpet for the closing ensemble, we stuck in a drum solo by Max. Sadik did not play on that record date.

If you had been at this session you'd be lucky to remember anything. I was like a policeman on duty—where's Miles, where's Bird, where's Dizzy? The only one who tended to be normal was Curly. Max stood around and took it all in. To him it was a floor show! For the next date with Bird we got Bud Powell on piano. You can really hear the youth of Bud here. I remember Bud in 1941 or 1942, before Cootie's band. We took him to Brooklyn one night and he drove everybody crazy. He couldn't count bars. The session was done at Harry Smith's studio in the penthouse above Steinway on 57th Street. And there was like a terrace overlooking the city and guys would go out on the terrace and get high. Again I had to play roundup. Keep my eye on the terrace, my other eye on the men's room and make sure nobody got lost. Harry Smith wasn't a great studio. I loved WOR—Doug Hawkins was a great engineer—but you know Herman was always looking for a bargain. Listening to Bird on successive takes is really something. The disciples like Sonny Stitt, great as he is, don't have the ability to go from take to take like Bird. Bud plays with great authority on this session.

In Detroit, I recorded the working group: Bird, Miles, Duke Jordan, Tommy Potter and Max. The engineer was Jim Syracusa and his studio was in the living room of a two family house. The echo chamber was in the bathroom. We had a session there once—not with Bird—when somebody used the toilet when the cutter was going. We didn't hear it until the playback, when all of a sudden you heard the flush!

The last two sessions with Bird were back in New York in 1948, during the second recording ban. The musicians came to the realization that they didn't gain anything from the first ban. The jazz guys simply said the hell with it, and made records anyway. The delegates were so busy checking Liederkrantz Hall or RCA on 24th Street that they couldn't cover everything. There were too many places to check. Like the studio in back of Schirmer's with the one-armed engineer. You had to ride a freight elevator to get to the studio. Union delegates were gentleman—they wouldn't ride in a freight elevator. Bird was under contract to Ross Russell and Dial, but

they'd had a falling out. I always stayed between Bird and
Herman. When I wanted Bird I'd go find him at 118th Street
and Manhattan Avenue. The dealings were between Bird and
me. Bird was my friend and Herman was just the creep I was
working for. Bird was always in money trouble. A lot of
sessions during the ban were the results of guys needing
money. Now I hung out with Bird, we were together all the
time. I'm still cursing him out for taking all my Marcel Mule
records. I had three copies of Ibert's Concertina de Camera
for Saxophone and Orchestra and Bird got every one.

I still get choked up listening to "Parker's Mood." Now,
Eddie Vinson was a blues specialist and he'd play the blues in
the good old way. But Bird! He'd take the blues and play
yesterday, today and tomorrow!

Bird listened to everybody and he'd wait for them to catch
up. Most of these things were heads—no arrangers, no
conductors, no batons. Bird conducted with eyeballs! Listening to this session you can hear how there was a serious side
and a playful side to Bird. Everything comes out in his playing!
Sometimes he'd get into nursery rhymes. Another thing is his

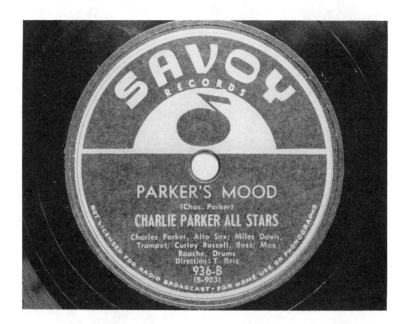

vocabulary. He'll drop into an older groove for three or four bars and then leap right back into the modern. Like shifting gears.

Bird was very businesslike with his music. He never prodded his musicians to get what he wanted, but he was firm in that he kept going until he got it right. Then he'd turn to Miles—like a father to his son—and say, "That was pretty good." I can see him with the big suspenders and the sweat pouring off him.

Everything in music comes from something else. There aren't any new notes. New rhythms, new interpretations, yes, but no new notes. So it was Bird the interpreter who really left a mark. He showed the way for Miles, Bud, Coltrane—all of it goes back to Bird. He was always a friend. I was happy for him when he went with Norman Granz because I knew Norman would pay him good money. He was my friend ever since I met him. It's hard to put my feelings in words. I'm not going to say anything derogatory about him because that has been blown up too much. That's all over now and all we have left is the music. That's Bird's legacy.

Charlie Parker *(Courtesy of the Institute of Jazz Studies)*

The funeral was crazy. The wives kept moving the body around from one place to another, but then Dizzy got Adam Clayton Powell into the picture at the Abyssinian Baptist Church. It was probably the biggest funeral ever in Harlem. I was one of the pallbearers. You've probably seen that famous picture coming out of the church where the whole coffin was on my shoulders. That was a sad day and that was a heavy coffin, but if they had asked me I would have carried it myself.

DIZZY

Dizzy Gillespie was the other great force in the forties. The musicians all used to copy him. I knew one little white trumpet player who used to follow him around. One day, Dizzy went to the barbershop—naturally it was one where the blacks went—and this idiot sat down in the chair next to him. When the barber asked him what he wanted, he answered, "Same as him." They copied Dizzy's clothes. He took my glasses and that was the beginning of the "bebop look." He grew a goatee and wore a beret, so everyone started doing it. But more important than the cosmetics was the music. People listened and wanted to hear more, even though they didn't know what the hell it was.

Basically, Dizzy is lazy, and he'll coast if he isn't pushed. That's why he carried Jon Faddis; that's why he bangs on the drums. But get him with a bunch of trumpet players, and he'll chop them down!

STAN GETZ: FIRST SESSIONS

One day I was hanging out with Harry Goodman, and we went to hear Benny at the Meadowbrook. They had moved the Meadowbrook from Cedar Grove to Symphony Hall in Newark because of the gas shortage. We heard this young kid playing tenor and he was sensational—a cross between Bird and Lester! I said, "I want him," and Kai Winding introduced me. I gave Kai the leader deal and gave all the white kids I knew a shot: Shelly Manne, Shorty Allen, Iggy Shevack,

Shorty Rogers, and of course Stan. After that session which was in January of 1946 I did eight more sides with Stan for Herman and then, when I got out of the clutches of Lubinsky, I signed Stan to Roost.

For Stan's first date as a leader I got one of my favorite rhythm sections: Hank Jones, Curly Russell, and Max Roach. Since Stan was so young I figured it would be a good idea to get him together with the section one time before the date. So I got the group a gig up at Monroe's on a Monday night. Stan was the leader and they all split the bread equally. Hank was making notes on all the tunes—he worked out all the intros, endings, etc. He gave everything to Stan, and Stan proceeded to leave all the music in a cab on the way to the studio, so they had to ad-lib it after all.

It wasn't hard to persuade Herman to record white musicians, even though 80 percent of his business in the radio store was black. A customer would come in with a radio to repair and Herman would tell him that he needed a new tube. Then he'd take the radio into the next room, shine up the old tube, give it back and charge $6. He was always looking for white

hopes, starting with Johnny Guarnieri and Herbie Fields. Allen Eager was very easy to sell to Herman. He had the Lester stance with the saxophone and his tone was reminiscent of Pres. To Herman, if you could do all that and you were white, you couldn't lose!

Herman also had an obsession with Lionel Hampton and boogie-woogie, so I told him I could get him Milt Buckner. Milt was red hot with Hamp and "Flyin' Home," "Hamp's Boogie" and so on. I approached Milt about doing a date for me, and he said he had a deal with Gladys and Hamp, who were getting up a label of their own. I said, "Look, we won't use your name—we'll call it the Beale Street Gang and you'll make a few dollars." So we did the sides, and they started to take off. We used to get records played by a Jewish wine distributor who sponsored a radio show. Believe it or not, Mogen David wine was a popular drink in the black neighborhoods, so this radio show could really move black records, and it created a big stir for the Beale Street Gang. Only nobody knew who the hell they were! People were desperate to book them, especially in the Washington and Baltimore area where

the wine distributor was based. Finally, Joe Glaser booked a group from California called the Beale Street Boys into the Howard Theater. They were a vocal group and didn't sound anything like the records, so they were fired after the first show. When Glaser found out what had happened, he didn't speak to me for a year.

In the midst of all the craziness with Herman and my own hustles, I tried to slip in a few of my buddies from Brooklyn whenever I could. I gave one date to pianist Kenny Watts, who used to give me rides back from 52nd Street. I used guys like Pazuza Simon and my friend Arthur Herbert, the drummer, on a date with Redd Foxx. Pazuza was a hell of a tenor player who was married to a shake dancer by the name of Flash Gordon!

Wynton Kelly was another Brooklyn guy. We used to go for breakfast at Bickford's on Nostrand and Fulton, where all the guys hung out. They used to hit glasses filled with water and make bets on which notes they were. Wynton was the judge, because he had perfect pitch. His first recording was on Savoy with Hal Singer in 1948.

MILESTONES

Miles Davis was another great talent that I'm proud to have given his first date as leader. I had recorded Miles with Bird, and even before that brought Miles in for a session with Rubberlegs Williams. I threw Miles into that date because Bird asked me to do what I could for him. Miles was a very nervous young man at that date. He had Freddy Webster, his idol, there to calm him down. After each take, Freddy would go over it with him. Herman didn't understand Miles at all. He pulled me aside and said, "Look, this is not a school! We don't have to have guys on the date with the trumpet player, trying to refresh his memory. We're in the record business; this ain't a goddamn university." Naturally, Miles hated Herman with a passion. Miles' first session as a leader came in 1947. I had promised Freddy Webster that I would try to help Miles. Give Miles credit; he had to put up with a lot working with Bird and really, like we owed him this date because of all the shit he took. Since Miles was still comparatively unknown, I felt that Bird's presence would help carry him over. Bird had a contract at the time that he didn't want to fulfill, so he conceded to play tenor on the records to camouflage his participation. I was anxious to record him on tenor anyway, since I always felt he should be heard on the instrument. He had played tenor in Earl Hines' band, but never recorded on it. He borrowed the horn one day for rehearsal and one day for the date. Miles was very serious about the session. He held rehearsals, and planned it all out. The first rehearsal, Bird went to the Braddock Bar and borrowed a tenor from Warren Luckey. I had to watch out for that tenor to make sure Bird didn't hock it! The second rehearsal was up at Nola's, which was over Lindy's. Bird showed up without a horn but he found some young white kid hanging around and invited the kid to come listen while he used the kid's horn. For the session I think he went back to Luckey. Even though he hadn't picked up a tenor since he left Hines, he sounded like he'd never been away.

ERROLL GARNER

One Savoy session I will never forget was when Erroll Garner produced his masterpiece, "Laura." We got to the WOR studios at 1440 Broadway only to discover that there was an elevator strike. Before we attacked the eighteen flights of stairs, someone got the brainstorm to pick up a bottle of brandy. Every few flights we would sit down and pass it around. By the time we got to the eighteenth floor, we were out of our heads. Afterward, Herman wasn't too thrilled about our doing something like "Laura." He wanted everything to be a boogie-woogie; he didn't know anything else. But from here on in I was beginning to get more control over things. I was even getting Mr. Lubinsky to stay away from recording sessions; I talked him into sticking with the business end.

PRES

When I first met Lester Young, I was more in awe of his conversation than his playing. He and Vic Dickenson had a language of their own, and nobody knew what the hell they

were talking about—it was unique. I met him at a bar, and then went to hear him with Basie at the Famous Door. Like everyone else, after hearing Lester once, you became a fan. In 1944, when Lester recorded for Savoy,[7] I didn't produce the date, but I did manage to deliver Basie. Then in 1949 I did some things with Lester on my own at Savoy. You may notice that there were a lot of good extra takes from the Savoy sessions. That was Mr. Lubinsky being cute. He knew he could eventually cash in on all those takes he didn't pay for. That's why he would often tell us, "I don't like that, let's do something else." As the years went by, he accumulated extra tunes. He was a shrewdy. In retrospect, I'm glad he did it, since now we have more Bird and more Pres!

"THE HUCKLEBUCK"

For a while I got out of jazz and into R & B, or rock and roll as it was later called. It gave me a chance to get away from Herman and to go to Detroit with a big expense account; I couldn't wait to spend Herman's money! I went out there in 1947 to check out a band that Herman had heard. I thought they stunk, but I liked the sax player, a fellow named Paul Williams. So I took him aside and told him, "Look fella, you don't know me and I don't know you. If you listen to me, I'll make you a lot of money. But you gotta do what I say—nothin' else. Don't even think." He looked petrified, but I kept pitching. "I don't want your band, I want you. I'll find guys for you to play with and the right material." So we rounded up some musicians and had a rehearsal. Paul started running all over the horn, and I jumped in and said, "Hey, I got Charlie Parker for that—I don't need you! Just give me that low B honk!" We almost had a fistfight right there. We sat around playing all those Earl Bostic things, and other King records looking for ideas. We used to hang out at a record shop at 3530 Hastings Street, and we even named a tune for that place, "3530," and recorded it in Detroit in the same place we did Bird. We stole pretty good and came up with a few hits.

Soon after, I went up to the Apollo Theater with Billy Shaw to see Arnett Cobb and Sarah Vaughan. Because of his health, Arnett had to cancel even though they had two more weeks in theaters already booked. I convinced Shaw to use Paul Williams at the next stop—the Royal Theater in Baltimore. Then I called Paul in Detroit and told him to get the six guys we recorded with, buy six gabardine suits ($50 tops), and to meet me in Baltimore. We rehearsed and got an act together. I taught him all the tricks—the honking, the kicking the feet. When they opened, we took the town over. The people were in an uproar, a frenzy. They tried to attack the band. We couldn't get Paul off the stage. I had to go and manually close the curtain. The guy operating the microphone started to lower it into the ground and I yelled at Paul, "Blow into it." He ended up playing on the floor; it broke the place up!

We walked out of there with a bundle. When I came home, I drove down Market Street in Newark and Lubinsky saw my '49 Cadillac. He only had a '48, so he figured I had robbed him. I set up a tour with Lucky Millinder, Bullmoose Jackson, and Paul. At a rehearsal in the Adams Theater,[8] Andy Gibson brought in a new arrangement called the "D-Natural

Blues." Paul and I both listened real carefully to this thing. Two hours later, at Paul's rehearsal, he's playing the shit out of it. I went to Andy and told him I wanted the tune. He said, "I can't. I got a deal with Lucky." Next thing you know, Lucky beat Andy out of some money, and Andy told me the story. "Do I get the tune?" I asked. "You got it," he answered, and signed the paper. Lucky was about to record the "D-Natural Blues" for Victor, and I'm ready to record Paul. We had to wait for the word from the union that the recording ban was lifted. Then we ran upstairs to Harry Smith's studio, by Steinway Hall. He didn't have an echo chamber, so I put the band in the hallway and recorded "The Hucklebuck" right there.

Of course it's almost the same as Bird's "Now's the Time," but we were real careful to change one note to make it different enough so we could get away with it. When the record came out I had all the black disc jockeys in my corner. When Lucky's "D-Natural" came out he said he didn't care. He told me, "I'm with Victor. What are you gonna do with that bullshit label?" I asked him to put it in writing, so he signed a paper stating that I owned "The Hucklebuck" and he owned "D-Natural Blues."

The thing really took off. I went to Tommy Dorsey and got Charlie Shavers to do it,[9] and after that Pearl Bailey and Hot Lips Page.[10] There was one line in the lyric that I fought over with the writer for hours. No one could say "sacroiliac!" Charlie Shavers did over twenty takes, and still couldn't get it right. Dorsey looked over and said, "I'm gonna try it one more time and if he doesn't make it you're gonna blow it." I said, "Give us two minutes," and took Charlie into a booth. I kept drilling him: "Sac-ro-il-i-ac,"—over and over. The next take we had it. When we did the version with Lips and Pearl, when she came to "sacroiliac," she turned to Lips and said, "You say the big word!" Then we got Sinatra to do it.[11]

Meanwhile, Herman and I got into a big argument. He went crazy because there was a trumpet chorus in "The Hucklebuck." He said, "That shouldn't have been in there; we'd have had a bigger hit!" I said, "How much bigger a hit can you get, schmuck!" So he fired me. Not that I minded. Thanks

to Paul Williams, I was in a position to escape from "Devil's Island," 58 Market Street, Newark, New Jersey—Herman Lubinsky, warden.

A few days later, Herman decided he wanted me back, so I made him pay a price. The best steakhouse in New York at the time was a place called Pietro's. In those days, a steak cost $13 and chateaubriand was $27. I made Herman buy dinner for me and all my friends, and to apologize to me. I was ordering cordon bleu like it was seltzer. Herman ended up with a bill that looked like a war debt! I went back to Savoy with a raise, and I didn't do a damn thing for six weeks. Herman kept bugging me, and I would answer him, "I'm thinking, Herman, I'm thinking." Finally he got the message, and I left Herman for good.

OTHER LABELS

Savoy was one of many small independents trying to make it in the 1940s. It was "monkey see, monkey do" and nobody had a contract. Nobody really wanted one. The artist wanted to stay free in case he got hot and got an offer from a major label. The owners, on the other hand, didn't want to make a commitment either. If you signed an artist to a year's contract, you would have to guarantee him twelve or sixteen sides. If you tried to get out after four, the federation could prevent you from doing any other dates until you lived up to your end of the bargain. Take a guy like John Lee Hooker. This guy was on 50,000 labels! Anyone with $100 in his pocket was cutting four sides with him!

Everyone was watching everyone else. The guys at the pressing plants would see where the demand was by the orders they got from the "race" shops. The small labels would then ape the big hits—like Apollo putting out Coleman Hawkins' "Rainbow Mist" after "Body and Soul" took off. There was a small company in Newark—Manor—that got started watching Herman and Savoy. I did a couple of things for them with Georgia Peach, and another with the Coleman Brothers. Of course, Herman was watching too, and if he thought he could build on something that was making some noise, he would. Like when Eddie Davis had a hit with "Lockjaw,"[12] we recorded him for Savoy. Herman only wanted medical titles! That's how we ended up with "Calling Dr. Jazz," "Fracture," "Spinal," and even "Maternity"! Otherwise he wanted everything to be "boogie." Whenever you see "boogie" in the title of a Savoy record, you know it's Herman. He also felt that having the artist's name in the title was a selling point. That wasn't my style, but I had to go along with it, even when it got ridiculous. On one Dexter Gordon session we did "Blow Mr. Dexter," "Dexter's Deck," "Dexter's Cuttin' Out," and "Dexter's Minor Mad." Just so you knew it was Dexter!

Most of the guys in the business were hustlers like me. Alfred Lion and Francis Wolf, who started Blue Note, were the exceptions. They were nice people and very sincere. In fact, they were such nice guys that I could never pull any of my stunts with them. Eli Oberstein, who had Varsity and Royale, was a different story. He was one of the most brilliant minds in the record business. He went over to Europe and bought up all those classical masters. He put out the first boxed sets, which he got from European radio broadcasts. He was a real manipu-

TENOR-SAX SOLO
LONG, TALL, DEXTER
(Dexter Gordon)
DEXTER GORDON QUINTETTE
Bud Powell, Piano; Curley Russell, Bass;
Leonard Hawkins, Trumpet; Max Roach,
Drums; Dexter Gordon, Tenor Sax
603-B
(Sav-5878)
Direction: Teddy Reig

CALLING DR. JAZZ
(Eddie Davis)
EDDIE DAVIS
EDDIE DAVIS & HIS BE BOPPERPS
Eddie Davis, tenor sax; Fats Navarro, trumpet;
Al Haig, piano; Gene Ramey, bass;
Huey Long, guitar; Denzil
Best, drums
Direction-Teddy Reig
907-A
(5-3367)

JUMPIN JACQUET
(Illinois Jacquet)
Featuring
ILLINOIS JACQUET
and his TENOR SAXOPHONE
with Emmett Berry, Trumpet; Fred Green,
Guitar; Bill Doggett, Piano; John
Simmons, Bass; Shadow Wilson, Drums
Direction Teddy Reig
593-A
(Sav-5871-2)

DEXTER'S DECK
(Dexter Gordon)
DEXTER GORDON
TENOR SAX SOLO
Argonne Thornton, Piano; Eugene
Ramey, Bass; Ed Nicholson,
Drums
576-B
(Sav-5842)

lator. He would print up one label for Sears and another for Montgomery Ward. One he'd call the Berlin Symphony and the other the Vienna Symphony, and it was the same fuckin' record! He was a master. Another hustle was perpetrated by companies like Melrose. Walter Melrose would pay for a record date just to get the tunes. The musicians might not get paid at all for the session, never mind the royalties, and a company like Melrose would build a huge catalog. This was before the days when the money went directly from the record company to the union to avoid that kind of thing. Of course the unions had their own thing going.

UNIONS

Almost everything the union did was aimed at creating work for the local men. Let's say you came from Kansas City to New York like Charlie Parker. You weren't allowed to work. You had to establish six months' residence without working as a musician. Then you could apply for a card. If you were seen blowing somewhere, you were in trouble. They tried to make it hard for good guys to come in. It still goes on in Hollywood. Urbie Green decided to go out to California. He couldn't get a job because the trombonists out there had a little thing among them.

Another rule was that if an out-of-towner worked seven days, he had to leave town. That was to prevent you from being held over. Once, while I had Charlie Parker booked at the Pershing in Chicago, some college kids approached me to get Charlie to do a concert. I looked at the contract, which was for something like two thousand. I added two-fifty for myself and said, "Okay, I'll call you tonight." Then I went out and got a nice bottle of Scotch and a bunch of cigars, and went over to the black union. I sat down with the president and went through the whole routine: "How're the kids, how's the dog? Have another drink, smoke another cigar." He gave permission for Charlie to do the concert. That's what it was all about.

Another rule to protect the locals was that when you played the theaters, every seventh week you had to have a local band, some of which were horrendous. I remember going to Baltimore with the head of the Gale Agency because we had booked Toni Harper, the little girl who had a hit with "The Candy Store Blues." The local band fucked up the music so bad that Tim Gale was about to have a fit. The second show was even worse than the first. I happened to pass by in the wings and heard Toni saying to the bandleader, "I don't know why you're having so much trouble—all you have to do is watch my foot." This guy is getting double scale as a leader and here he is being taught time by an eleven-year-old girl!

Some unions did nothing at all except take their cut. In Newark and Philadelphia, if the guy came around to check cards I'd tell him how many guys we had and he'd tell me what the "tax" was. I'd give him the money, plus five for himself. Petrillo held Chicago like a gorilla, but that was the white action. He didn't care what the blacks did.

New York was mob controlled. Everything depended on who you knew, and you could get around any rule. In the dime-a-dance joints they'd work them eight days a week if possible for $20. There was a rule that you had to have a day off every seven days. When Duke Ellington went into the Cotton Club, they'd book him for eight weeks but he only played seven. The extra week took care of the days you were supposed to have had off each week. Sonny Greer once tried to stand up in front of the tough guys with the cigars and said, "No! I want a day off every week." They convinced him he didn't really want a day every week.

Well-connected owners held the scales down for years. It was all political. The union would hand out plums. If a guy was out of work, they'd give him picket duty for $6 a night. But if a club paid off, they never had to worry about pickets.

I learned how to circumvent a lot of the corruption, and I always tried to be straight with the musicians. When it was a shitty deal I would explain to them, "Maybe the bread ain't right, but you ain't doin' nothin' so you might as well take it." I wouldn't use my friendship with a musician to get him to do something cheap as a favor.

CHAPTER FIVE:
ROOST

IN THE LATE 1940s and early 1950s, I continued to make the club scene whenever I could. The joints were constantly changing owners and names. A lot of these transactions were less than friendly. The Royal Roost was originally a chicken place which didn't work out. So Monte Kay, Symphony Sid and Ralph Watkins turned it into the Roost and brought jazz to Broadway. The club was very successful, but then there was a split and some guy who was a big shot in the checkroom business came along. It was sold to some uptown numbers bankers and they tried to turn it into another Cotton Club. A club named Bop City opened where the old Zanzibar and Hurricane used to be. Birdland was originally the Ubangi

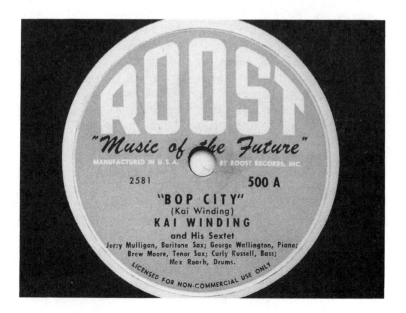

Club, which was run by the mob. The Ubangi was another miniature Cotton Club, with a lot of girls on stage. Sammy Kaye and Irving Alexander took it over. Sammy had been a partner with Ralph Watkins in Kelly's Stable on 52nd Street. He was married to a dancer named Zorita, who was famous for performing with a snake around her neck. Then Monte Kay and Morris Levy put up a few dollars and got involved with Birdland, which was named for Charlie Parker. One night we all went out for hot dogs and came across a Filipino with a bunch of birds. We got the bright idea to buy up all these birds and put them in the club. The next day, the guy who cleaned the place turned on the air conditioner, and that was the end of the birds. In 1950, I got involved financially with Birdland because Irving and Sammy had an argument. I bought their end of the option period on Erroll Garner and worked out an arrangement whereby Erroll went into the Apollo and Birdland. The club's operating money had run out, but we eventually beat a guy for $900, and that's how we kept Birdland going.

Roost Records actually started one night in a club. I had done pretty well with Paul Williams, and one night I came back off the road with a bucketful of money. A bunch of us were sitting around the Royal Roost, stoned to the bone. I said, "Let's chip in $1,000 apiece and open a record company." So Ralph Watkins, who owned a piece of the Roost, Symphony Sid, Monte Kay and I each put in a thousand. Although I was the ringleader I only had eight hundred, so I owed the two. And that's how Roost Records was born—in a drunken moment.

Our first date for the label was almost a disaster. I had set up a session with Kai Winding, Gerry Mulligan, and Brew Moore. Some of the guys had a problem in those days, and it turned out that, due to circumstances beyond their control, they couldn't make the session. I had no credit and had to pay for the WOR studio up front. I had also paid the union, so I had to do a date or lose everything. So I ran uptown and got my dear friend Mario Bauza. We rounded up the Machito orchestra and Harry Belafonte, who were working at the Roost, and did "Lean on Me" and "Cubop City."

BUD'S BUBBLE

Some of the most influential recordings issued on Roost were the eight sides by Bud Powell. They weren't done for Roost originally, but for the Braun brothers, two chicken farmers from Linden, who owned DeLuxe records. I grabbed Max Roach and Curly Russell for the date, and we did four sides in an hour and a half. I asked Bud if he wanted to do four more, since we had a lot of time left. He was happy, because that meant more bread. But Max wasn't satisfied, so Bud came over to him and said, "What are you complaining about? I'm doin' all the work—you're just keeping time." Max started to pack up. Finally we cooled the whole thing out and they made history on that day. Despite what Bud said, if you listen to those sides you'll hear that Max really holds the whole thing together. That rhythm section laid the foundation of much of what came later.

I had a little falling out with the brothers from Linden. Using the charm for which I'm famous, I slammed one of them against the wall, ran in the back, grabbed all the masters and split. That's how we got the Powell sides for Roost.

MOONLIGHT IN VERMONT

Our biggest seller on Roost was guitarist Johnny Smith. The main problem was his name. How does a stone-cold hustler like me deliver a name like Johnny Smith to the public without people wondering whose identity I was hiding? When I explained the problem, Johnny said, "You're not going to change my name, are you?" I told him no, even though it was a nice name to check into a motel with. I knew we had to get him together with somebody with a name to get him over the threshold. I had Stan Getz under contract, so we paired the two of them and "Moonlight in Vermont" was the result. No matter how long you're in the business, it's impossible to predict what people will like. Don't believe any producer who tells you, "I knew it was going to be a hit." Nobody knows; like

with "Moonlight in Vermont," it just happens. I knew I liked it and I could only hope the people would too.

Johnny went on to make over a dozen albums for me. One day, at the end of a session, we needed another two or three minutes to complete an LP, so I asked Johnny if he had anything in his head. He came up with a thing called "Walk, Don't Run," which has won two BMI awards and made six figures—almost as much as I made out of Roost.

SONNY STITT

Sonny made a shitload of records during his career, but I always felt his work on Roost was among his best. Bird had a deep affection for Sonny, but they had a clash over some money from the "Marmaduke" session we did in Detroit. Bird took it upon himself to punish Sonny by blowing directly at him for the whole date of eight sides. Afterwards, Bird and I were sharing a cab back to the Mark Twain Hotel and I asked him, "Why'd you do Sonny like that?" And he said, "Somebody's got to teach him. He can play, but he's crazy; he's gonna mess up." Anytime Bird said someone could play, I listened. So when I got my own label, I tried to feature Sonny in the right way. I always felt Sonny and I had a personal rapport which brought out his best on records. I tried to team him with top arrangers like Johnny Richards and Quincy Jones, and that gave him a framework so he really had to come out and play. Incidentally, that was the first time Quincy got arranger credit on a cover.

By the late 1950s, I was into all kinds of different things. I got involved in some rock and roll, managing Chuck Berry. I even took a trip down to New Orleans to find Dave Bartholomew, who wrote all those things for Fats Domino. While I was down there, Wynonie Harris and Roy Brown happened to be in town at the same time. I got the brainstorm to have a "battle of the blues." To hype the concert I got Wynonie to go to the club where Roy was singing. Roy always had his big Cadillac parked on the street out front where he could keep an eye on it. To stimulate the "battle" I convinced Wynonie to jump up and down on top of the car. All at once

ROYAL
ROOST

"Music of the Future"

MANUFACTURED IN U.S.A. BY ROOST RECORDS, INC
(1108)
Capitol Songs, Inc.

JOHNNY SMITH QUINTET
Play
MOONLIGHT IN VERMONT

Featuring
Johnny Smith, guitar; Stan Getz, tenor; Eddie
Safranski, bass; Sanford Gold, piano;
Don Lamond, drums.

547

JOHNNY SMITH
AND STAN GETZ
Moonlight in Vermont

ROOST

catalog. In between, we did a few things for Reprise and Columbia.

The first thing we did for Roulette turned out to be one of the most famous—the album with the bomb on the cover.[13] Neal Hefti was one of the writers that really knew Basie, and that album proved it. The band was working in Pep's in Philadelphia. They were a hot attraction with Joe Williams and "Every Day." Neal went to Philly to start writing, but at the Philadelphia date we never had the regular band. All the trumpet players were sick, so I was juggling personnel constantly. I ended up sending Emmett Berry and Lammar Wright, and all the older guys who could see a chart and take care of business. So, with all the substitutes, when it came time to do the record date, the band had never really played the music before. Neal conducted, and history was made.

It's funny, but because of the precision of that band, everyone always assumed we played the charts constantly before a recording session. The truth was that in 15 years of recording Basie, the only date for which we had the music in advance was *Chairman of the Board*. That was taken entirely from the book, all things by the "homies," Frank Foster, Frank Wess, and Thad Jones.

With all due respect to Neal and Basie, I must give credit to my wife on "Li'l Darlin'."[14] They just couldn't seem to get it right when she pulled Bill out of the control room and said, "Cap, y'all got this tune wrong!" And she hummed it at that slow easy tempo. Basie said, "That's it!" He hurried back in, got the guys together, and they did it.

While we're giving out bows, I'm going to take one for "The Kid from Red Bank."[15] That one was to be a feature for Bill, who suddenly decided to become a society band pianist. I walked up to him and said, "What in God's name are you doing? This is a boogie-woogie thing. Give me some ya-ta-ta! Elbows, knuckles, you know!" And Basie went back to the piano like he was going to show me up. And he did the whole bit—with the elbows, fists. When the take was over, I grabbed the mike and yelled, "Cap, you're a general!"

I know I have an ego, but I think I contributed to the sound of the band over the next few years, and I think Basie knew it. The Basie orchestra was built on playing together.

That was the chemistry. I was old enough to remember the original Count Basie band of the late 1930s and early 1940s when Jack Washington would lean over and pass a riff to Lester; Lester would pass it to Earle Warren, and the first thing you knew, the five saxes were leapin'. Then the brass would get a counter thing going. I tried to get that kind of togetherness; they had to sit one on top of the other and feel each other. We weren't looking for stereo effects by having the guitar in left field, the bass in right field, the drums in center field, and the piano in the dugout.

Basie himself was the catalyst, and I always realized that. After I left, when he brought in arrangers, they would usually take over stomping off the tempos, etc. Or he'd have Marshall Royal (who we nicknamed "the Bürgermeister") kick things off; then the band would sound like the Casa Loma Orchestra. But Bill would be very happy because that gave him less to do. My gimmick for beating Basie at this game was to have the arranger include piano introductions. Basie would always look at those charts and say to the writer, "I can see Teddy's been influencing you—you wrote nothing but piano intros!"

Even though he didn't like to take charge, Basie could assert himself when the occasion demanded it. When we recorded the "Li'l Ol' Groovemaker," which was a thing Quincy Jones wrote on "King Porter Stomp," for some reason the saxes just couldn't get in at the right spot. Things were getting a little tense as the clock was winding down. I said, "Bill, we gotta get this thing cleared up so we can go home!" So Basie said to the band, "Just follow me, fellas." And at that exact spot on the record, you can hear Basie cue them with a big "choink" at the piano. The saxes came in like clockwork and we finished it in one take.

An example of what Basie meant to the sound of the orchestra can be heard on a date we did without the band: the *Memories Ad Lib* album, with Joe Williams. On that one Basie plays the organ, and you can hear him convey the whole foundation of the band sound by himself.

With the growing success of the band, guys wanted more money, and there were new union laws to contend with. Instead of riding on a bus for three hundred miles, you had to take a plane. The costs kept going up and that led to some things I'm really not too proud of, things like the Jackie Wilson and Kay Starr albums. But when you have someone at a record company who's willing to shell out $10,000 for Basie's services alone, and to pay for all the charts and copying, plus a taste for me as producer—well, I couldn't exactly say no. In addition, I felt it was important to get Basie into the pop field. The jazz clubs could barely seat twenty people, never mind a band of twenty men. So I had to get him into bigger places.

One thing I was proud of was the Basie-with-strings album, which was my idea. The first tune was "These Foolish Things." As soon as Basie heard the strings, he started playing dinner music at the piano. Naturally I got all upset, and was about to go into my act, when Willard Alexander stopped me.

He laughed and explained that years ago Basie used to play at the Ritz-Carlton in Boston. He learned that you play differently for people who are eating than you do at the Savoy Ballroom. And when he heard the strings, he automatically went back to that style. So I got him in a corner and said, "What's this shit Willard's been telling me about you and the Ritz?" And he looked up with that devil-in-the-eye smile. I said, "Bill, just because there are strings you don't have to become Carmen Cavallaro!" In spite of that, if you listen to "These Foolish Things," it still has the Cavallaro flavor. One thing that I was very happy about on that date was "Song of the Islands." Joe Mooney used to have a group with clarinetist Andy Fitzgerald. Andy used to do Lester Young's chorus from the "Song of the Islands" record by Basie. Andy did it on bass flute, so on the Basie string date we had him play it and when he got through, during the playback everyone stood up and applauded.

I'll be the first to admit that some of the stuff we did—especially pairing Basie with other "stars"—didn't work out. The date with Sammy Davis, Jr., was a real fiasco. The cost of the album was ridiculous—around $46,000. No date cost that much in those days. The band was in Detroit, and Sammy added voice in New York. The record company executive is crying on the phone, "Can't you cut a corner?" I said, "What can I do?" The union man was there all the time. Finally, when he called back for the twelfth time, Basie said, "Let me talk to him." Basie listened to his sob story and said, "Well, you know we'll try anything we can to please you, but we can't violate the union rules. I tell you what, though. Teddy and I are going to the racetrack now and I'll put twenty on a double for you, and if it comes in it's yours!"

By the time the Sammy Davis session was ready to be mixed, I couldn't stand to listen to it any more. How many times can you listen to the same music over and over, when you know it's going downhill? It reminded me of the only date I ever walked out on. It was with Chris Connor. I left poor Don Sebesky in the studio with little bits of tape all over the place, trying to make sense of the code numbers. We were cutting in four bars at a time. I just didn't want to go through that with Sammy.

Another mismatch was the date we did in 1968 with Jackie Wilson. There was a lot of trouble even before the session because I wanted to use Benny Carter as arranger. Benny of course was my favorite, and he had written *Kansas City Suite* for Basie which was one of the greatest things we did at Roulette. His writing on *The Legend* was also terrific, but I never liked the recording quality; we couldn't use the studio we wanted. Harry Garfinkle at Decca told me, "I don't think you should use Carter; he's too old-fashioned." I blew up. "If Benny Carter's old-fashioned," I yelled, "your mother's a whore and your father's a faggot, and fuck you!" I went over to Decca and tore up the contract, even though I needed it badly. I had booked the date so that Decca would pay to transport the band to Vegas. Willard Alexander and Basie himself intervened and I finally got my way.

A funny thing happened at the session. We were doing the Sam Cooke song "Chain Gang," and Jackie starts singing it like it's a Christmas carol. So in my discreet way, I went into the control booth and told him, "Listen, this song's about a guy who just came out of jail. His dick's hard and he's goin' to get some pussy. You're singin' it like a faggot!" When I walked outside, everyone's in hysterics. They had left the mike open and every word went out all over the studio.

Our term with Verve was a bust. The only album that got off the ground was the *Li'l Ol' Groovemaker*. But in the meantime we had hooked up with Sinatra and Reprise. We booked Basie into Atlantic City on a Friday night, and met with Frank to set up the deal. We discussed it for a while and shook hands. The agreement was that we do one album with Sinatra and one for ourselves. I had been pretty tight with Frank from before, but that night I really got to see him operate. I remember he didn't like the bread the restaurant served at dinner, so he sent someone to Philadelphia to a bakery for some rolls.

I had enough clout with the Reprise people so they let me run things without interference. I saw this as my chance to get Basie into the pop field. We had done an album for Roulette called *Dance Along with Basie*, which was the direction I wanted to go in. At that time we were hindered by budget, and the record never got any attention. So now we came up with

Count Basie *(left)* and Benny Carter, 1961 *(Courtesy of the T. Reig Collection)*

Hits of the Fifties and Sixties, which had the band doing their own versions of pop hits. Right after the date, the band went on vacation. When we went back on the road, the band started playing some of the new tunes. You could see an immediate reaction in the audience. They were pushing up to the stand, really digging the pop stuff.

One of the last things I did with Basie was one of my favorites: the live album in Vegas in 1969.[16] That one came about strictly out of necessity. If you stay in Vegas long enough you go broke, and that's what happened to us. I had to figure out some way to meet the payroll. I got ahold of my good friend Tom Mack, who always wanted to do a Basie album of all the old standards—something that would be an evergreen item. Then I went to the people at the Tropicana and submitted my plan: let us record every day for three days. You can publicize it, people can come and you set up a bar for a nightclub atmosphere. We can each earn a dollar and have a ball. They went for it, Dot records went for it, and we were on our way. I brought Wally Heider in with a truck to record it. My favorite thing on the record is "Blue and Sentimental." I got the idea from an album called *Tutti's Trumpets* on Disney's label.[17] Toots Camarata had written out a lot of the great trumpet solos, but for five trumpets. So I said, "Let's do 'Blue and Sentimental' but instead of doing the tenor chorus like it's always been done, let's do it with the whole sax section."

I was always trying to broaden the market for Basie, and we set up a big date with Petula Clark at Purdue University. She was hot with "Downtown" at the time. Once again, I almost blew the whole thing with my big mouth. When the band was in Hollywood, she came to see them play. At one point, Miss Clark's husband turned to me and asked, "Can they read music?" With my usual tact I responded, "You asshole motherfucker! You think those music stands are footstools, prick?" And I walked away. The next day, my phone kept ringing. It was her agent; she wanted to apologize. I didn't want to hear any of it, but my friend Mike Gould prevailed upon me and I gave in. They took me to dinner at the Coconut Grove. I ordered a slew of those pineapple-banana cocktails. I ate chicken in a coconut shell and all kinds of shit and got completely crocked. I apologized to Petula Clark for my outburst and language, but I explained that Mr. Basie was not just a client but my dearest friend. When I got back to New York and sobered up, I was still seething. I ran into Lou Levy, who was the publisher of "Downtown." I told him I wanted a favor. I wanted to do a parody of "Downtown" with Joe Williams and Basie. He said, "I got a million-dollar copyright and you want to jerk it off? I don't care how you get back at her, just leave me out of it!"

We had a much more pleasant collaboration with Fred Astaire, with whom we set up a TV special. Astaire was the most dedicated and meticulous performer I have ever met. We brought him a bunch of Basie records so he would pick out things he could work with. He chose a medley on "School Days" that was in the book at the time. What he didn't realize was that when a band plays a chart for a period of time, little things get changed. Eventually, it's not the same as what was on the paper or in this case the record. Astaire had hired a famous Hollywood choreographer, Hermes Pan, and he had something cued for every beat. Only when we ran through it, nothing fit. So we ended up having the band synch to the record for the show.

In 1958, through Mike Gould, Basie got the opportunity to do the theme for the TV show "M-Squad." Mike apologized, "It doesn't pay much, but it'll be good for Bill." When he heard that Basie would only get a thousand, Willard Alexander went crazy. I explained that Bill would be the writer, and would have money coming in all the time from it. We finally agreed to go ahead. This was to be the first black orchestra to do a theme for television. The press came out in full force, along with all the wheels from the union. All the big shots are standing around shaking hands in the studio and waiting to hear the music. The truth was we had nothing. After an hour and forty-five minutes, all the executives started looking at each other. So I took Bill into the men's room and said, "You know we're fucking up." He said, "It's O.K., don't worry about it." He went back to the piano, gave one of his signals, and all the guys start running to their chairs. Then he motioned to Thad Jones to come over. Basie played a couple of chords, mumbled something, and sent Thad back to the trumpet section. Then he conferred with Marshall Royal, and

he delivered the message to the saxes. The next thing you know, we had "M-Squad." And Basie was the sole writer.

ELLINGTON-BASIE

The truth was that Basie never really wanted to do the date with Ellington. He had nothing but love and respect for Duke, and didn't want any session that would hint at competition between them. But because Morris Levy had used Ellington with Louis Armstrong on Roulette, Columbia made demands for something in return. So we settled it by making the album of Basie and Ellington together for the first time—both pianos, both bands, everything! We used four charts from each band, expanded for the two orchestras.

The one condition that Basie demanded was that they not make it into anything like a battle of the bands. They wanted to name the album "Battle Royal," which was one of the tunes Duke brought to the session. Basie said, "No way," so they ended up calling it *First Time Out*.[18] Basie was in awe of Duke and used to refer to him as "the master, the creator." Sometimes when Basie's band was at its peak, and Duke had lost some of his stars and was having his problems, Basie made sure not to lay it on too thick if the bands were playing the same neighborhood. There was nothing but love between them, and this album was a labor of love—plus getting out of a contract obligation by Morris Levy.

The session was done at Columbia's 30th Street studio, and boy, was that a sound! Basie and Ellington were having a picnic at the pianos, putting each other on. Duke would pick up on Basie's last note and go on from there. As they shifted from one to the other, nobody knew who the hell was playing. Teo Macero, who produced the date, admitted that he was having trouble differentiating between them. I ended up standing between the two pianos to cue the engineer.

Basie and Ellington were two completely different characters. You could enter into a conversation with Bill, but when Duke got through talking to you, you didn't know what the hell he wanted. After the session, Teo asked Count and Duke if they would each say a few words at the end of the record. Basie looked at me and shook his head, so I said no. Then Teo asked, "Well, how about some pictures?" Again Basie said no. Later, in the car I asked him what that was all about. "I'm not gonna fuck with Duke," he answered. "He'll start talking some shit and I'll sound like I never went to school." Then I asked about the photos. He said, "Now I know you're crazy. Duke'll put on some costume that'll make me look like I never owned a suit!"

It took a lot to upset Basie. With all the crap we put him through he just thought of himself as "the piano player" and took it all in. He left all the yelling and screaming to me and, I must say, I handled it pretty well! But once in a while, Bill would get upset. For example, we did two albums for Command under the supervision of Bobby Byrne. Their game was stereo effects, and I've never been so ashamed of an album in my life. It sounded like it was recorded in the subway. At the session, Basie exploded. He was always a master at protecting his men's chops, especially the brass players. He knew how to pace the program at a dance or concert so that the guys would have a chance to recover after a flag-waver. He would either noodle around at the piano for a while, or choose something easy. And at recording sessions, he liked to get things in as few takes as possible. Well, at this Command thing, after every take Byrne kept yelling, "Yeah! That sounds great. Let's do one more!" At one point Basie finally stood up, closed the piano, and yelled, "For what?" Byrne got the message and shut up quick.

Another time he got upset was when we did the Basie-Tony Bennett album at Columbia.[19] If you can find one note of Basie on that record I'll kiss your ass! Basie didn't like the way Mitch Miller was running things. Again, he kept wanting to redo perfectly good takes on the first tune. Ralph Sharon was also at the piano, so Basie looked at me and said, "They don't need us." So we split.

Basie hardly had any trouble with the guys in the band because they respected him so much. He was no pushover, however, and could keep them in line in his own quiet way. For example, when we were opening at the Waldorf, Bill was approached by Al Grey, known throughout the industry as "Local 802" because he knew all the rules and regulations. Al says to him, "I need a draw, chief." So Basie asks, "Well, is it draw day?" "No, man," Grey answers. "But I gotta get a pair of shoes to go with my tuxedo for tonight." Count looks at him and says, "Tell you what, Al. I'll take out all your solos, and then you can wear those brown shoes you got on and no one'll see them!" That night, Mr. Grey appeared in a pair of black patent leathers that must have been buffed by seven laborers!

On the rare occasion when he really got mad, Basie could be devastating. We were doing a bunch of one-nighters and Al Hibbler was the singer. One night at a restaurant Hibbler made the mistake of stealing the lady of the evening away from Bill Basie. Hibbler of course is blind, and every night after his set, someone would always come on stage to escort him off. So

at the next performance, after Hibbler finished, Basie jumped up from the piano and said, "I'll help him." So he took Al by the arm and walked him backstage right into a wall! Al ended up sitting in a pile of mops and brooms.

As I said, Bill wasn't one to complain; he usually took whatever came his way. As far as the artistic matters went, he rarely took much of an interest in planning any new projects. If I really went too far with some of my cockamamie schemes, though, he would gently let me know that enough was enough. The only time he asked me to set up a particular kind of album for him was the session with the Mills Brothers. He really enjoyed working with them, and you could feel the happiness there. I eventually was able to arrange it for Dot. The first album we did was wonderful, but then they wanted us to rush out another one in time for their sales meeting. The band wasn't going to be in New York and Dick Hyman, who did the first album, wasn't available. So it was done multi-track in Chicago, and then sent to Los Angeles. I objected to the whole procedure, but Bill was happy and the money was good.

Basie was basically a straight arrow with an old-fashioned sense of propriety. He once refused to appear on a bill with Dick Gregory because the comedian was doing "racial" jokes. In the 1950s, I went out to the Coast with him, and Lenny Bruce was working the same club. Basie called Billy Eckstine and said, "You worked this joint. What gives with that white guy?" Today it would be nothing—Richard Pryor makes him sound like a minister. Another time I had set up a party for Basie to meet with a bunch of deejays. A few of them lit up and Bill disappeared. Knowing Basie, I went right for the kitchen because he would always get tight with the cook. Sure enough, I found him and asked him what he was doing in the kitchen when there was a party going on for him. "Shit," he says, "I'm not gonna be in there when they all get busted!"

He had a terrific sense of humor and a unique way of describing things. One night, someone announced that they were going to the drugstore, so Basie says, "Bring me a bottle of Ben Webster." Nobody knew what the hell he wanted until it dawned on us that he meant a bottle of Brut cologne; of course Webster's nickname was "Brute."

Bill tried not to show his emotions too much, but he was

deeply affected by the loss of his friends. I'll never forget when I broke the news of Art Tatum's death. He sat there for a long time, then looked up and said, "You know, it's a hell of a thing when a guy dies. It's a hell of a hell of a thing when a guy dies and he's your friend. But it sure is a hell of a hell of a thing when a guy dies, he's your friend, and he takes all that talent with him."

Maybe the most revealing thing about Basie was the way he treated his retarded daughter. Even though it was a tremendous burden, he and Catherine refused to put her in an institution. They insisted on caring for her at home. Once, Edward R. Murrow wanted to do a show on Basie, where they come in and go all over the house. Even though he could have used that kind of money and exposure at the time, Basie refused to let them into his home, because it might mean hiding his daughter someplace while they shot.

SARAH VAUGHAN

Although Basie occupied most of my time, I worked with a lot of other artists at Roulette. Sarah Vaughan had always been one of my favorites, and when she became available, we signed her. Sarah was a hangout buddy of everyone's—just one of the cats. Apart from the usual settings, I tried to record Sarah in some challenging surroundings. I always remembered an album Ella Fitzgerald did with only the backing of pianist Ellis Larkins. So I went to Sarah and said, "On this next album I want you to sing naked." She said, "Are you losing your mind?" "I want you without all that jive noise," I explained. "Just you and a simple background—whatever you feel comfortable with." She said, "How about guitar and bass?" I said, "Great. I want George Duvivier." "That's great," she answered. "And I'd like Mundell Lowe." I said, "You got a deal." So we set up a studio with a bar and a gang of food. Sarah invited all her friends, and we set up comfortable chairs for everyone. When she felt like making a side, she did it. It was a ball, and I think it resulted in one of the most relaxed of Sarah's albums—*After Hours*.

Later we went out to California and I teamed her with my

favorite arranger, Benny Carter, for an album called *The Explosive Side of Sarah Vaughan*. Of course Benny is famous for his reed choruses, and he wrote a beautiful one on "I Can't Give You Anything but Love." While the band ran through it, Sarah was walking around trying to get a feel for the chart. When she heard the reed chorus, she started to sing along with the saxes. Benny and I immediately looked at one another and decided right there to have her sing the lead part with the reeds.

There's an interesting story behind one of the records we did with Sarah. One day, Jimmy Jones, Sarah and I were picking material for an album,[20] and Sarah came up with "Have You Met Miss Jones." I said "Great," but I didn't pay any attention to the lyric, which was actually written for a man.

When I realized it at the studio, I took some liberties with it to make it fit. I knew this was illegal, so after the date, I went up to the publisher, Chappell, with an acetate. I explained the whole thing to Stan Stanley, the manager, thinking I might have to scrap it. Stan said, "It's so good, let's send it over to Richard Rodgers himself and let him decide." Later I got a message to call Mr. Rodgers, and he told me, "If you have any more artists that want to mess up my songs the way Sarah Vaughan messed up 'Have You Met Miss Jones,' you have free license to do so!"

CHAPTER SEVEN:
LATIN INTERLUDE

AFTER BASIE AND A FEW OTHERS left Roulette, we ran into some financial problems and thought that Latin music might be the way to go. I'd always loved the music anyway. So we picked up an affiliate label called Tico, and did some Latin things. I could do these sessions for scale. First, I grabbed my friend Mario Bauza and Machito and did an album called *Machito's Back*. We also did a lot of double-entendre songs with Miguelito Valdes and Machito, as well as some folk-type music.

Mario Bauza was the man who introduced me to this music. He played trumpet with Chick Webb's orchestra. Webb assigned him to look after Ella Fitzgerald—to keep the wolves away. Mario later went with Cab Calloway. We became friendly, and he kept telling me he was going to get together an orchestra with his family back home in Cuba. Frank Grillo (Machito) was his wife's brother, and Mario formed the Machito Orchestra. I met Machito when he worked with Miguelito and Xavier Cugat. Southern Music was the agency that booked all these Cuban bands; actually, "enslaved" is a better word. They'd bring a guy over to join Cugat and treat him like a migrant worker! They paid him and then took back all the money for food and other expenses.

Dizzy is one of the guys that learned about the music from Mario Bauza. Both of them played together with Cab Calloway, and when Dizzy formed his big band, thanks to Mario, it had a great Latin influence. Dizzy is one of the few guys who can handle all of those complex rhythms. Mario brought in the father of the conga, Chano Pozo. After the job, wherever they were, Chano would get out a hat box and Dizzy would put his mute in four pillows, and they would play together and pick each other's brains. From that friendship came great things like "Cubano-Be," "Cubano-Bop," and "Toccata for Trumpet." Chano was what you might call a rogue. He got involved in some kind of swindle in a bar and as a result, he was laid out on the sidewalk. When it happened, I grabbed a cab and ran downtown to pick up Mario. He threw himself on top of Chano's body, crying.

Miguelito Valdes absorbed all the teachings of Chano Pozo and once he got away from the Cugat "plantation," he had some big hits at Victor. Another kid they brought up from Cuba was Daniel Santos. He was a real giant but nobody heard of him.

There used to be a little Spanish music shop on 51st Street and 6th Avenue. I used to wonder what went on in there. There was never anybody inside, yet they stayed in business. So one day I tiptoed in and found the owner, a Mr. Perez. He had a little label which issued all those older African chants from the Cuban hill people. Through those records I found Arsenio Rodriguez, who knew all the African religious things. He played a guitar called a "tres," which had three double strings. It sounded like a harpsichord. I found out that he was blind and lived in some government housing in Cuba. In those days I would fly from Miami to Havana for $18 to buy cigars. I noticed that Havana and New Orleans were the only places I had been where the bars never closed. There was music all around. If a guy was playing one of those black Cuban flutes, another guy would start banging his ring against a glass. The bartender would start beating something with an ice pick. Pretty soon all these rhythms would start blending. The cook would even stir the soup in rhythm!

All these things stayed in my head, and I made it a point to get to know Arsenio. And when I got involved in the Tico label, I recorded him on one album which never did too much.[21] But I heard something in him. We signed Tito Puente and Eddie Palmieri, two giants in the Latin field. Tito is a genius at combining jazz and Latin music. He reminds me of Jimmy Mundy. They both had a way of hearing things and filing them away for later use. They may not have been his, but he sure knew how to use them! I recorded an album with Eddie Palmieri called *Azucar* (Sugar).[22] I used to call him the

Latin "Monk." Like Thelonious, his voicing of chords was unique. I also found a kid who played the fiddle and the Cuban flute. His name was Pupi Lagarreta. You never heard music like that!

We also brought in Ray Barretto with a band of four fiddle players and rhythm. We had a little hit which was the prelude to "rap" records. It was called "El Watusi" and involved two guys engaged in a conversation. Nobody knew what the hell they were talking about. There was only one word in English at the end, and I used that to fade on.

I came across a lady they called the queen of the Cubans: Olga Guillot. I tried to sign her for Roulette but there were a lot of problems. She had a communist background. She wasn't actually a communist, but she had to join certain organizations just to exist. Because of that, getting her in and out of the country was nearly impossible. Today, when she appears in Miami she plays in stadiums and holds ten thousand people in the palm of her hand. She has such electricity!

Another great Latin performer I worked with was named Lupe. She was full of fire and rhythm. When she sang, she used to tear her clothes, her jewelry would fly off, and everyone would run all over chasing the beads and things. Nobody could handle her. I put together a little musical marriage of Lupe and Tito Puente. The first album we did was a smash hit on the Spanish market.[23] When Lupe started to warm up, Morris Levy got interested in signing her. Morris could speak a little Spanish, so they got together in his office. I sat off to the side, trying to stay out of it. By this time, Lupe felt she was a real star. She looks at Morris and says, "Mr. Levy, I know you want to fuck me!" So she opens her pocketbook and says, "Here! Go ahead!" I almost fell off the chair! Lupe was really insane. She got into religion, and then it was all downhill. Before we could do a second album, she hurt her back in Puerto Rico. When she returned we had to take her to the hospital and put her into traction. Tito Puente was involved in voodoo and had a lot of faith in the "padrino," or high priest. We went up to visit Lupe at St. Luke's and Tito tells me to stay outside her door as a lookout. After a while I peek in and there's the padrino taking Lupe out of traction! He takes out a bunch of candles and starts praying over her and rubbing her with oil. I was also praying—praying that no doctor came along and had us all arrested! All this didn't do a thing for Lupe. In fact, the padrino convinced Lupe that she was going to die. Meanwhile, we needed another album, so we did it with Lupe lying there in the studio like a mummy. Someone had some painkillers, and by the time we were done, she was foaming at the mouth. I was lucky we didn't end up with a murder rap.

Around this time, Morris Levy was trying to make some Spanish shows happen at the old New York Paramount Theater. I got Miguelito and some others in there, but then Joe Glaser sold Morris a bill of goods. He ended up with Cugat. Having Cugat on that show was like bringing Guy Lombardo into the Apollo!

One of my last acts at Roulette was to sign Chick Corea, but he never made a record there because I left the company. I went over to Verve and did a lot with Willie Bobo.[24] It was a fusion of Latin pop and jazz. But the greatest thing we did for Verve was something called *Patato y Totico*.[25] Patato [Carlos Valdes] was another Cuban, and one of the few who could play the conga correctly. He brought in all the authentic musicians. We had the bass player Cachao [Israel Lopez], whose family had a long classical history in the Philharmonic in Cuba. Totico was the singer Juan Drake. We had a rehearsal for the date and to me there was something missing. So I told Patato I would record it, but I wanted to bring in Arsenio Rodriguez. He went along with it. I was very proud of the results, but unfortunately the company really didn't know how to operate in that market. But it was so good that the Cubans in Miami bootlegged it and sold thousands and thousands of copies. Chico O'Farrill brought his son to the session and told him, "I want you to pay close attention, because this is the sound of Cuba we may never hear again." I was very proud to be part of that.

Soon everyone was incorporating some type of Latin rhythm. Johnny Pacheco, who played bongos and congas, was one guy who got a lot of work. He was light-skinned and good-looking, so he could get on the networks. Tony Bennett used Candido for a while. Eydie Gormé knew how to speak

PATATO y TOTICO

Spanish and did a couple of Latin albums that were bigger than anything she did in English.

Unfortunately, so many of the original Latin giants, like Arsenio Rodriguez and Rene Hernandez (who was the pianist and arranger with Machito) never lived to see their art gain recognition as such an important part of American music. People still don't realize how deep the Latin influence goes.

CHAPTER EIGHT:
CODA

In 1963, Basie went over to Verve. MGM had bought the jazz catalog, and that was my first experience working with "conglomerate mafia." Everybody was getting a taste, so no one could snitch. We had Connie Francis, Jimmy Smith, Stan Getz . . . big sellers. We had to produce sales figures daily. The sales guys would offer $300 suits to the distributors, just to get things moving. Another game was free records. The distributor would buy a thousand records and get five hundred free. Then he'd sell the five hundred, and send the thousand back. Then the accountants came up with some "Chinese arithmetic" about royalties. They decided that we would use "extended" payments over a ten-year period, and convinced the artists that it was better for taxes. It was Herman Lubinsky all over again, only much more sophisticated! What eventually ruined the catalog was that they would print records like toilet paper, and then sell them as cutouts.

By 1970, I was having a lot of health problems. I had bad arthritis in my hip and they had to shorten my leg. I had to walk with a cane. It was hard for me to go into New York and have everyone look at me and say, "Oh, I'm so sorry." I'd think, "What are you sorry for? You had nothing to do with it." Anyway, I stayed home; I became a hermit.

After a while, people kept telling me to get back in the business. I guess it's like a virus that gets into your blood. The clincher was when my kid kept telling me that my records were old-fashioned, that everyone I liked was dead, and so on. So I decided to enter the electronic age. I had run across a piano player—another Cuban—named Jorge Dalto. I met him at the recording date Dizzy did with Machito for Norman Granz.[26] I liked what I heard, so I talked to him. He was complaining about everything. I said to myself, that's good, because you can't make a nickle with someone who's compla-

Teddy Reig *(Chuck Stewart)*

cent. We made an agreement, shook hands, and suddenly I was working again. It opened my eyes to a whole new way of recording,[27] and I didn't like what I saw. I really didn't know what I was getting into. First you put the rhythm down. Then you add the horns. The whole thing dragged on and on. I had never heard of plugging in something when a guy plays bad. It took twenty-four hours just to mix it! I couldn't help thinking that with all the new technology, the soul was lost. Just note the differences from the studio to live performance, especially in rock. The artist can't do on stage what he did in the studio because he doesn't have twenty-two chances.

I thought back to the conditions under which we recorded Bird and the others in the forties, and what happened was really a miracle. We had to balance the instruments right as they came in. Sometimes, for example, you can hear the piano get real loud, as the engineer realized that a solo had begun. If it took more than one pair of hands, I would help out by bringing up the bass, while the engineer did the piano. There was no going back and making adjustments; you were stuck with what you had, and it better be right. You had to pamper the engineers or they'd really screw it up. An artist would spend a lifetime developing a sound and an engineer could destroy it in ten seconds.

Some artists grew attached to certain microphones. The studio itself was important—the wood, the floors. You had to know the different studios; you had to keep the blueprints in your head. Columbia had Liederkrantz Hall, which was a dream. It had a natural ambience and all the musicians loved it. After the engineers redid it, it was never the same. Then Columbia got the church on 30th Street. They were swingin' their asses off in there until the engineers got ahold of that one too.

In the 78 era, time was everything. As I said before, the worst thing was watching that clock run down to about 2:30 or 2:45; you never knew if they were going to finish in time. I used to have cardiac arrest during that last fifteen seconds. Some of the real giants—Count Basie, Benny Goodman and Benny Carter, for example—had built in metronomes. No matter how many takes you did, they would never vary more than four or five seconds. The time was so crucial because when you got to the smaller part of the disc, the louder tones would break the groove walls. You had to be real careful with the bass, because the jukeboxes were overloaded with bass. When you sat in a bar, that thump would come up through your feet! After a while, the wall of the record would break down. If a jukebox owner kept having to replace a record, he'd stop putting it in there.

As if things weren't fragile enough, during the war years, there was no metal and no shellac, so they came up with glass discs. When Josh White made "One Meat Ball" for Asch, they brought the disc to Symphony Sid at his studio, so he'd play it on the air. I used to hang out with Sid, and happened to be there when Josh White, whom I knew from his days in the Village, came by. I spotted a chair and sat down. Suddenly I hear a big crunch; I had destroyed the disc! Luckily they were able to run back to the studio and get another copy cut in time for the broadcast.

Even if you did everything right, you were still at the mercy of the pressing plant. We used to get a lot of bad pressings, and it was important to determine whose fault it was so you'd know who'd make up the cost. Was it the plating? Was it in the cutting of the mother to the master, or in the actual pressing?

When we started using tape, it relieved a lot of the tension. But it had its own problems. Early tape used to stretch easily and if you weren't careful, the pitch would change. Tempo was still important if you were doing any kind of splicing. Also, when LPs first came out, we still tried to keep it to two and a half or three minutes a track so you could make singles for the jukeboxes, plus a 45 and a 78. You tried to get the most mileage out of each recording. Tape also created a feeling on the part of the artist of, "Well, fuck it. I'll come back tomorrow." Somehow, "tomorrow" never happened right.

When stereo first arrived, everyone was looking for effects. They would build fences around the musicians. Basie had the perfect answer. He used to say, "We sound better in toilets!" By that he meant that it might be crowded, but the band could feel one another. Again, it was a chemistry. When I went into the studio with Basie, I used to act so crazy that none of the recording people wanted to be near me and we could set up like we wanted.

Most important, you had to remember that you were dealing with human beings with chops. Guys couldn't keep hitting a high note indefinitely. Basie knew all about that. After they played a rocker, he would noodle around for a while or make a speech, just to let them recover. He did the same thing at a recording session. He wasn't just wasting time. You had to consider each individual. For example, Charlie Parker hated the microphone. You had to know how to get him up to the mike without making him self-conscious.

When I began in the record business, there were people around who knew something about the music. Today, you don't talk to music people; it's all in the hands of accountants, lawyers and technicians. If you say you want sixteen strings, they tell you to get a synthesizer. On the other hand, the artists could be unrealistic. You try to accommodate their ideas, but if they don't agree to bend at all you're going to have problems. The artist may forget that someone's putting up cash money. You've got to get that money back with a profit, or you won't be making records for long.

Even the album covers have become ridiculous. They used to have something to do with the record; now they put butterflies on the cover. Chuck Stewart is one of the best jazz photographers and contributed so much. I remember him from the days when he was Herman Leonard's assistant. There's been a lot of attention paid to black filmmakers and photographers lately, but nobody seems to mention Chuck.

Jazz has always been mistreated by the record companies. Every few years there's a resurgence of jazz. All the companies jump into action and scrape up all the garbage and repackage it. The next thing you know, there's an overflow in the stores and they start complaining that jazz doesn't sell. And it dies again. Then somebody comes along and creates a little stir, and the whole thing starts all over. It will be that way until the music gets its due respect. They don't take all of the classical music out of the catalog; it lives forever.

I may sound bitter but I'm really not. The last few years, since I got sick, have given me a chance to spend time with my family and to reflect on things. I was truly one of the lucky ones. I spent my life living and working with some of the true geniuses of our time. Genius takes many forms, and I just tried to accept these people on their own terms. A genius does things his own way. For example, I once brought a concertmaster of the Philharmonic to hear Stuff Smith. He's staring at Stuff, who's jumpin' all over the joint and he keeps saying, "It's impossible! It's impossible!" I bring Stuff over, and the guy starts asking him to make certain notes on his violin. Finally, the concertmaster asks, "How do you make a G with your finger here? It just can't be done!"

Some people have so much talent that they operate in a different world. I used to try to have a conversation with Thelonious Monk. I remember one night I sat with him at a bar listening to Eddie Heywood. I bought him a drink. Suddenly he jumps up, thanks me for the drink, and runs out the door yelling "Jess Davis music, that's what it is!" And do you know what it was like to sit and talk with Bud Powell? I learned that if a guy is that much above my intelligence level, I just leave him alone. What am I going to discuss, sex? Certainly not music!

I think you can see from the kind of records I did that I don't like to categorize, or emphasize any particular style. I like anything that's played right. Sometimes I'm amazed and flattered that people study so seriously the stuff we did years ago. But the basic thing is that it makes you pat your foot, sing along, and feel good. Never mind the labels, the sleeves and the covers. Go for the music; be happy with the music.

Teddy Reig *(E. Berger)*

Talking about Teddy

LEONARD GASKIN

Bassist Leonard Gaskin was born in 1920, and became a close associate of Teddy Reig's in Brooklyn. Part of the 52nd Street scene, Gaskin was an important contributor to the developing bebop movement of the 1940s, working with Dizzy Gillespie and Charlie Parker. He participated in many historic recording sessions, including Reig-produced dates with Don Byas, J. J. Johnson, and Allen Eager {Savoy}, Erroll Garner {3 Deuces}, and Stan Getz and Sonny Stitt {Roost}. Gaskin also introduced Teddy to Ineta Forshee, who would become his wife. In the early 1950s, in addition to his jazz activity, Gaskin worked as a staff musician at CBS radio. From 1956 to 1960, he was a mainstay of Eddie Condon's group. His varied activities in the 1960s included recordings sessions with jazz luminaries Miles Davis, Zoot Sims, Al Cohn, and Stan Getz, and pop stars Elvis Presley, Bob Dylan, and Dionne Warwick. Gaskin continues to play regularly in groups led by Doc Cheatham and Big Nick Nicholas, among others, and has presented many educational programs for the non-profit International Art of Jazz organization.

I DON'T REMEMBER EXACTLY when I met Teddy, but I was with a little amateur band at the Bedford Ballroom in Brooklyn. Teddy would be there often. There was another ballroom he used to frequent—the Sonia. Many of the big bands used to play at those places, and he met a lot of the musicians—such as Willie Bryant, Cozy Cole, and many others. Teddy was a pretty forward fellow and because he was so easily identifiable by his size, he became well known to all of the musicians—those who were established as well as the up-and-coming ones. We all used to hang out in a restaurant in Brooklyn after the clubs closed.

When I began working on 52nd Street, I believe it was the latter part of 1943, Teddy and I would ride back and forth on the subway together. We were very close and became even closer when he became affiliated with Savoy Records and Herman Lubinsky. Before that, however, we were friends in the days when his mother and father had a candy store on Blake Avenue. I knew his parents, too. They wanted him to become something "legitimate" but his first love was music. I would go up to the store and his mother would ask him to take his turn working, but Teddy found hanging out with the musicians and the nightlife more interesting. Of course there would be some yelling and his parents would make quite a scene. He would come and hang out at my house. My father and I lived together in a big house in Brooklyn. Teddy would arrive and wake me up. He was a very warm fellow, and he and my father would sit and talk for hours, sometimes all night.

Teddy was a hustler even then—before he actively pursued a career in the music business. During World War II, when records were very scarce, he used to show up at places with stacks and stacks of them. He never explained where they came from. There were many characters around at the time. The section of Brooklyn in which Teddy lived was a real melting pot. Many of his associates like Bob and Mort Shad and Jack Hooke came from there.

On 52nd Street, Teddy started hanging out with the "hip" musicians. He used to visit the 3 Deuces when Ben Webster had a group there in late 1943. I was working further down in Kelly's Stable on the next block. There were twelve clubs just on those two blocks. Teddy was friendly with everyone. He became very close with Sammy Kaye and Symphony Sid. This led to the formation of 3 Deuces Records. He even got me to contribute $500, which was quite a lot of money at the time. I got it back eventually and even made a few bucks on the deal.

INETA

I introduced Teddy to his wife, Ineta. She was a friend of mine. Her maiden name was Forshee and I knew her whole family who were also from Brooklyn. When they moved to Manhattan, my friend Otto Wilkenson and I continued to visit them. A few years later, Teddy, Otto, and Jimmy Lockley started to sponsor jam sessions. They called themselves the "JOT BOYS"—Jimmy, Otto, and Teddy. However, to get back to the story, in Netta's building there was a guy who took bets on "single action," a form of betting on the numbers resulting from certain horse races at the track. I would listen to the radio in Netta's apartment, then run down to the basement and put an eight-to-one bet on the right number at the last minute. He never discovered my method. Anyway, Ineta used to come to places where I performed and Teddy would be there too. As they say, the rest is history. They fell in love and were married. Netta became more and more Teddy's focus. Teddy and Netta had their share of racial incidents, especially when they moved to Teaneck.

Teddy was always getting into trouble. Some of it was his fault because he was always challenging somebody. He had a brash nature, and instead of letting something go, he would pursue it. Occasionally, things would get nasty. We were involved in a few incidents where, if he had just said, "Forget about it," it would have been cool. He would confront anybody. On one occasion, he had a run-in with a policeman who called for reinforcements. They took Teddy off to the 17th Precinct. I had to find Lubinsky to get him out of jail! Despite the fact that Teddy had had a number of ribs removed, which made him very vulnerable, he still challenged everyone.

IN THE STUDIO

Teddy was always in favor of integrating the recording groups with which he was associated. He really didn't have any prejudice. But, unfortunately, there was often a misunderstanding among the musicians. Some of them thought Teddy took advantage of them. Even when I tried to explain what was going on, they were adamant. At times I would think, "The heck with it." I knew the problems weren't Teddy's fault; he was just caught in the middle. In order to understand the situation, you had to know Herman Lubinsky, who was a character just as Teddy was a character. Teddy saw Herman as a way of making a living. To Herman money was his god. If he could beat you out of $5, that was a great achievement! When

Teddy first started working for Savoy, Dun and Bradstreet listed Herman's worth, as a major stockholder at Bamberger's, at $10 million. Herman was a real shrewd dude. He would buy electronic parts for two cents and sell them for five. Or he would respray radio tubes and sell them as new. Anyway, Teddy and Herman had this thing going with each other. Teddy would get the musicians and then the session would run too long. Herman would say, "I'm not going to pay any more money for this." Teddy would be in the middle, and the musicians would get an attitude. I would often end up in big arguments about Teddy. I remember being on one of the Don Byas Savoy sessions. We were going overtime and Herman says, "How much you want for the next half-hour?" So Don says, "Just give us a jug." That did not sit well with the rest of the guys but, what the heck, we were already there so we never made an issue of it. We all knew what Herman was, and that was the end of that. He was so engrossed in his money that he gave up his family. He lost them all. Teddy finally disassociated himself, but I remained around Herman for years, during which time I did almost every gospel record he ever made. After Teddy left Savoy, Lubinsky got crazy. He became "knowledgeable" and tried to deal with the musicians. When that didn't work, Ozzie Cadena came in, but he didn't have the rapport with Lubinsky that Teddy, and later Freddy Mendelsohn, had.

I remember hearing about Teddy's first date, the Rubberlegs Williams session with Bird for Continental. I knew it was Teddy's because Clyde Hart discussed it with me. Teddy and I were traveling back and forth together from Brooklyn at the time, and he gave me a copy of the record when it came out. When Teddy did a date, he had to do everything. He had to gather the guys together and get them in condition to play. Then, in the studio, no one wanted to take the initiative, so he'd decide on a tune and we'd try to put it down on wax in a given time. Teddy didn't know anything technically about music, but he managed to lead even when he didn't know what he was leading. Since no one else knew what was going on, Teddy had to sound authoritative to the sponsor he had talked into backing the date. So he's got the musicians and the engineer to deal with and, of course, the time. No one ever made time. If you had a date called for one o'clock, some musician would stroll in at one-thirty or two. Teddy generally handled all of this very diplomatically. He'd take the guy aside and say, "You know, you're letting me down." He could be very adamant with shopkeepers and policemen, but not with musicians!

There is a story about another one of Teddy's dates. It was Vido Musso's first session as a leader[28] and Teddy had called Leonard Hawkins to play trumpet. Vido had the music written, and Leonard could read very well, however, at that time he was strung out. Leonard took one look at the music and said, "Too many notes." He packed up his horn, walked out, and went to the movies! Vido Musso swore that Leonard Hawkins had made him blow the biggest opportunity he ever had to make a hit! What could Teddy do in a situation where the guys were irrational?

I was on a date Teddy produced with Frankie Socolow which was total chaos. It was Frankie's first date[29] and the trumpeter Freddy Webster was on it. We did a tune called "Reverse the Charges." A controversy arose because Freddy wanted to play ballads to show off his tone, and Frankie wanted to do something rhythmic. Teddy was the A & R man and somehow he had to deal with the situation. It took a lot of negotiating. I remember recording with a one-armed engineer that Teddy used, but that was not for Herman. I did some sides for a fellow we used to call "the thief of Baghdad." His name was Ben Bart and he had the Hub label. And, yes, the engineer would get blind drunk!

ERROLL GARNER

In October of 1949, I was a member of Erroll Garner's trio. Teddy was the manager. We flew out to Detroit for our first road trip—Teddy, drummer Charlie Smith, Erroll and myself. We had just left the Deuces, and had also been doubling at the Apollo Theater. Erroll had become a big star. When we arrived, Teddy rented a Dodge—a tiny thing. I was used to seeing Teddy in those great big Cadillacs. Big as Teddy was, that Dodge looked like a kiddy car. Teddy and Erroll used to love to go into a store and order all kinds of silly things. They just threw money away! They bought cameras they had no idea how to operate, and lenses they didn't even know how to put on. There was plenty of money and Erroll used to pass it out freely. Then we'd go through another scene where they blew all the money and I had to pay the plane fare!

Teddy produced a date we did with Erroll on which we did a tune called "Through a Long and Sleepless Night I Mention Your Name."[30] We had a rehearsal somewhere. Rehearsing with Erroll was a trip because we would say, "It's all set now," and then everybody would get lost! I believe it was a double session, so a great deal of time was involved. We finally got together for the last hour or so, and all the rehearsing didn't mean a thing. We did it all differently.

If not for people like Teddy, the history as we know it would not have been. His sessions turned out so well because he was a friend of all the guys. He was spending his nights listening to us, and his days hanging out with us. That made a difference. In those days, the musicians were distrustful of people. Working with an outsider wouldn't have had the same ambience. Today, recording has become a business. Then, it was new to everyone involved. It wasn't all figured out. Now we go into a studio, read a part, and just play it. Then, it was listening to each other, feeling each other, empathizing with each other. The camaraderie was beautiful. Looking back, we often refer to those times as every day being New Year's Eve. We never knew what would happen or where we'd wind up.

Teddy was an integral part of it all. On the outside he was brash and boisterous, but people never knew how sensitive he was on the inside. I can only say that in my dealing with him he was very fair, very warm, very loving, very giving. You can rest assured that he gave me more than I was able to give him.

3 DEUCES

(10010)   Piano Specialty

THROUGH A LONG AND SLEEPLESS NIGHT
(Mac Gordon - Alfred Newman)

ERROL GARNER TRIO

505

Erroll Garner *(Courtesy of the Institute of Jazz Studies)*

GUS STATIRAS

Born in 1922, Statiras has been a fixture on the jazz record scene since the mid-1940s. After working in different capacities for other companies, he launched his own label, Progressive, in 1950 with important sides featuring Al Cohn and George Wallington. The label was reactivated in 1975 when Statiras produced a series of superb LPs by such luminaries as Hank Jones, Lee Konitz, Buddy DeFranco, Sonny Stitt, Flip Philips, and Tommy Flanagan, among others. He continues to be active as a producer for Jazzology Records, as well as issuing Progressive material as part of the George H. Buck catalog. Statiras also runs several jazz parties nationwide.

I MET TEDDY REIG UP IN Harlem in the mid-1930s. I got to know a lot of hardcore jazz fans from the Bronx and Brooklyn up there, and Teddy was one of the Brooklyn guys. We'd run into each other at places like the Savoy Ballroom, the Renaissance, the Hotel Theresa, the Golden Gate, the Baby Grand, and Small's Paradise. I was just a teenager trying to learn the lindy hop and looking to hang out with musicians. One of my most vivid memories of the period was going up to the Savoy in September of 1936 to hear the Jimmie Lunceford band. Everyone was jumping so much the floor bounced up and down and the dust flew two or three feet in the air! Some of the young ladies of Harlem took my friends and me in tow and showed us how to jitterbug. I remember seeing Teddy around in those days. He was very enthusiastic about the music and was a good dancer. There were a lot of heavyweight fellows who were light on their feet like Teddy; they looked like feathers when they started to dance.

I didn't really get to know him until a few years later, when a very active jam session scene had emerged. Around 1940, Monte Kay, Pete Kameron and Jerry Weiss (who later changed his name to White), decided to run regular jam sessions on

Sunday at Kelly's Stable. Teddy was a close associate of
Monte, Pete and Jerry. Harry Lim had already started his
sessions at the Village Vanguard on Monday nights. He later
switched them to Sunday afternoon. About the same time,
Milt Gabler started his jam sessions at Jimmy Ryan's. Harry
Lim's sessions used to have guys like Sid Catlett, Nat Cole,
Coleman Hawkins, Lester Young and Ben Webster. Many of
these same musicians were also featured at the Kelly's Stable
jams. I wanted to catch a different crew, so I would go to Milt's
sessions to hear the "Condon gang." He also had people like
Frankie Newton, Emmett Berry, J. C. Higginbotham, Sandy
Williams, Albert Nicholas, and the guys from the John Kirby
group. There was more variety at Milt's sessions. I became a
good friend of Milt and of Jack Crystal; I was a regular
customer at their Commodore Music Shop. The knew me as a
young kid interested in jazz. After I'd been dropping in there
for a couple of years they hired me. I worked as a clerk
alongside Jack Crystal and Timme Rosenkrantz. Everybody
used to come into the store and I got to know a lot of people in
the business. My family lived in Jersey City, but my father
always owned luncheonettes in the Times Square area. I had a
car—a 1937 Pontiac—and it was real easy to come into the
city.

 We young jazz fans knew where all the record shops were
located. We used to go all around New Jersey, as well as New
York. One place we used to visit was the store Herman
Lubinsky owned in Newark: United Radio. This was before
Teddy started working for Herman at Savoy. The store carried
records, but was primarily a radio tube shop. In downtown
Manhattan, around Cortlandt Street, there were a lot of good
places to buy records. They used to call it "radio row," and
we'd scour these places for used records. I remember one in
particular—Sam Coyne's on the corner of Greenwich and
Cortlandt, where the World Trade Center is now located. In
his basement he had tons of jazz records from jukeboxes.
We'd wait around until they brought in a new shipment and
buy whatever we wanted for 7 cents apiece. All of us jazz
lovers would run into each other at these places. Two of the
collectors we used to bump into were Ahmet and Nesuhi
Ertegun. They'd come up from D.C. to search for records.

Almost all the guys we hung out with were traditional or swing fans; they hadn't yet gotten into "modern" music. Teddy was a "pusher" of the new stuff, as were Monte Kay, Pete Kameron, and Jerry Weiss. Teddy put it on record; the others should get credit for promoting it in a jam session context. We were all taken by the Jay McShann records with Charlie Parker, however. They once got Charlie to come to one of their sessions at Kelly's Stable. Teddy was there, and of course he became one of Charlie's biggest fans.

By 1945, when I was in the army in California, I started hearing Teddy's name in connection with record production. By then, I was involved with Bunk Johnson, along with Bill Russell and Gene Williams. I recorded Bunk in New Orleans in January of 1945 and, by the time I got back to New York, a lot of people knew about it.

In 1949, I got a job with Abbey Records. We were located on 50th Street and 10th Avenue. It was record row—all along 10th Avenue from about 44th Street to 56th Street. There was one record company after another, as well as jukebox operators and distributors of all kinds. Pete Dorraine had started Abbey as a Jewish party record company. It was named for the Hotel Abbey. Nothing much happened with the Jewish records, so they hired Ted McRae as an A & R man. McRae was a saxophonist who had been with Chick Webb and had an "in" with all the big bands. He brought along a friend of his named Gene Novello, a songwriter who stuck to Ted like mustard plaster. Novello put up the money for Abbey and became a silent partner. Our secretary was Aretha Robinson, who had written a lot of blues songs in the 1920s and 1930s. We also had a songwriter named Frankie Davis; he actually only wrote words because he couldn't write music. He had been around for years—one of those "Brill Building types."

I was doing a lot of commercial things for Abbey: rhythm and blues and country and western. At the time, they were known as "race records" and "hillbilly records." Most of them were terrible. Pete Dorraine hated black artists and jazz musicians! We fought constantly. In fact, the very first date I did was all black, with some important jazz figures. I recorded a girl singer, a friend of Ralph Cooper, the emcee at the Apollo Theater. We had an all-star rhythm section, including Calvin

Jackson on piano, Oscar Pettiford on bass, and I believe Max Roach on drums. I got Johnny Griffin on tenor and the string quartet from Toscanini's orchestra. The two tunes were "Until the Real Thing Comes Along" and "The Nearness of You." Brick Fleagle did one of the arrangements and Calvin Jackson the other. A lot of jazz fans don't know about that one.

One day I came to work and found the door padlocked. I went out to Long Island to talk to Pete Dorraine, who told me we were $60,000 in debt. I told him I thought I knew a way to get us back in business. I'd heard something on the radio that I couldn't get out of my mind. It was a transcription of "The Old Piano Roll Blues," which Eddie Cantor had made for the Red Cross. I'd memorized the melody and words and sang it for him. I thought it could be a big hit as a jukebox record—just what we needed. He thought I was insane, but agreed to do the recording. My idea was to get the piano roll company to do a roll for us and then we'd add a banjo, guitar, alto sax, and rhythm section with five male and five female voices. I had the whole routine worked out. Meanwhile, we checked with ASCAP and BMI and no one had a record of who the composer was. By sheer coincidence, Cy Coben wandered in while we were working on it. He practically jumped through the ceiling, yelling, "I wrote that song! I just gave it to Eddie Cantor to do for the Red Cross!"

Just before the session, they sent me on the road, promising that they would record it just as I'd planned. Instead, they used two singers. They did get a guy to do the piano roll. He was J. Lawrence Cook, who worked as a postman at the 34th Street station during the week and went up to the QRS company in the Bronx on the weekends to make piano roll masters. "The Old Piano Roll Blues" was released under the name Lawrence "Piano Roll" Cook.[31] I was down in Nashville, Tennessee, and they airmailed me an acetate. When I heard it I almost fainted because it wasn't what I wanted. I managed to get it played on the air and sold thousands of records in Nashville, Memphis, Birmingham, Atlanta and Charlotte. By the time I got back to New York, it was number twelve on the Hit Parade! With the money he made, Pete Dorraine was able to buy a building on 48th Street. I came in one day, and there was my name on the door of an office, with my own secretary.

They'd also hired Kelly Camarata, Toots' brother, as my new boss. Well I didn't need a secretary and I certainly didn't need another boss! I was supposed to have gotten $10,000 if the thing became a hit, but I never saw the money, even though I'd bailed out the company. So I got pissed and left.

I went to work for Herman Lubinsky at Savoy in 1950, but only lasted about a month. The first thing Herman told me was that he wanted me to make him another "Piano Roll Blues"! I wasn't interested in that, but I'd lined up a date with Yank Lawson and Bob Haggart and one with a young piano player named Dick Hyman. Lubinsky cancelled both dates for no reason. Lawson and Haggart went on to do fifteen albums for Decca, and Dick went to MGM and became one of the most in-demand pianists. Then Herman said he'd pay me $250 a week to hang around Dizzy Gillespie and Charlie Parker and convince them to record for him. Of course, they would have nothing to do with him—I can't repeat what they told me to tell Herman!

Working for Lubinsky, even briefly, I got to see what Teddy was up against. With the budget Teddy had to work with, he did some amazing things. Lubinsky would try to get five tunes done in the time allotted for four. You paid the musicians for three-hour sessions. Right after the war, scale was $21.25 for a sideman, $42.50 for the leader. Lubinsky never went by union rules. He paid ten dollars, fifteen maybe—whatever the traffic would bear. And he'd pressure the A & R man to get that extra tune out of the musicians, so if you did two dates, you got five records instead of four. BMI paid Lubinsky every three months. They sent a sheet about fifteen feet long which had all the tunes Herman had published on Savoy. He had me check all the titles with smaller amounts beside them to see if he was being cheated!

Everybody was thinking up new ways to make a buck back then. I got involved in helping singers to make demo records and with writers who wanted to make records of their tunes. I even started a label for one record! I called it Arrow Records. Some fellow who wrote songs had a girl friend with some money and I recorded them with a group called Four Beaus and a Peep! I was doing all kinds of things on the side. I was in the studio so much that I didn't see sunlight for days at a time.

In the spring of 1950, I worked for Bob Weinstock of Prestige setting up his distributors on the West Coast and down South.

I saw that I was helping everybody else and finally said, "Why not do it for yourself?" I started my own label, Progressive, in 1950. I was very close to Teddy at this time. He'd started Roost a couple of years earlier and we'd swap information about the business. Teddy and I never felt we were in competition because we each had our different artists. There was room for everyone. Jazz fans would buy anything if it was good. Teddy had an office in the Brill Building, and we used to eat together at the Turf.

Teddy was great to talk to and always had a new gimmick in mind to put over a record. He knew all aspects of the music and publishing business. He'd learned a lot from Herman Lubinsky about collecting royalties on tunes. The music business was not just records; it was publishing, as well as club and theater dates. The records would help promote the artist and get him jobs in the various venues.

As independents, we hated the distributors because we could never collect any money from them! You'd make a good side and ship a hundred copies to Chicago or Detroit and you wouldn't get paid for months. To the distributors, jazz records were relatively slow sellers, so they were in no hurry to pay up. And they always had the option of returning unsold inventory. So it wasn't like any ordinary business where you sell something, you get paid, and that's it. You could never rely on a steady cash flow. Meanwhile, you were committed to new sessions.

I always got along great with Teddy, but I saw him make a lot of enemies. There was one episode that took place outside Bob Portem's, which was located on 11th Avenue and 50th Street. Portem was the distributor for all kinds of jazz labels in the early 1950s. I was in there one day seeing how my records were selling, when Teddy pulled up in a white Cadillac. Teddy was there to collect his money or sell some records, and when he tried to leave he couldn't because there was a big truck blocking his car. Teddy went berserk and took off after the guy with a Coke bottle! That same afternoon, Teddy told us that he'd made a ton of money betting on a Yankee baseball game the day before. It seems he'd paid a girl to spend the previous night at the Warwick Hotel with the pitcher of the opposing team. Teddy got her to wear him out to the point that he could barely throw. The next day, the poor guy was scheduled to start against Whitey Ford and, not surprisingly, he was knocked out in the first inning. Teddy made a killing!

By 1956, I'd moved down to Georgia, so I rarely got to see Teddy. It wasn't until I started up Progressive Records again in 1975 that we renewed our acquaintance through Bob Porter. We spent a long time reminiscing about Harlem and the old days in the business. Teddy was still scheming. He had just put out some Charlie Parker-Ella Fitzgerald things on his Natural Organic label, and we were going to do something with some other masters he'd been saving. But as much as I liked Teddy personally, I didn't want to get involved with him in a business deal. The reason was that I had a connection in Japan and this company wrote to my attorney in New York saying, "If Gus Statiras has anything to do with Teddy Reig, we will terminate our business dealings with Mr. Statiras!" I never told Teddy of course.

In 1976 and 1977, Teddy was really pressing me to work with him on some deals. I'd listen to him, but I'd explain that I had so much cooking that I couldn't take on anything else. He'd try to convince me by saying we'd make a dollar today, and fifteen million tomorrow! He could talk you into anything! I was fortunate in that I was down here in Georgia, so I had an excuse. By this time, he no longer had entree to the big companies. He had hurt himself with a lot of guys in the industry and they didn't want anything to do with him. He got so frustrated at one point that he threatened to throw a guy out an office window when he wouldn't deal with him! Then Teddy's wife died, and he was completely devastated. He called me and we talked for a long time about how lonely he was without her.

In his last years he used to tell me not to talk to interviewers who wanted stories about our experiences. He'd say, "Don't give them anything! Write it down, keep it for yourself, sell it!" I used to tell him, "I have nothing I want to keep. Why not let someone else know what happened, if it can help them?" In 1983, he called me with a proposition. "Gus," he said, " I'm going to get a nice new Cadillac, and you and me are going to go around to the colleges and talk about the recording industry and all the crazy things that happened on our record dates." He told me, "All these people are giving lectures about their trips to Africa. What we've got to tell is much more interesting!" He thought we could get $5,000 each per lecture. I said I'd be happy for a couple of hundred! He was trying to relive the old days, where you get a car and go on the road—like the bands used to.

Who could guess that forty years later all of this would be of interest to anybody. We were just trying to make a living with the music we loved. We never thought that the fact that you saw someone in a club on a particular night should be noted in a diary! As far as the records we made are concerned, I did have it in the back of my mind that some day they would still be considered great. We felt a little like crusaders.

JERRY WEXLER

Jerry Wexler joined Atlantic Records as a partner and producer in 1953. His contributions to the rhythm and blues field are legendary. The long list of artists whose careers he helped shape includes Ray Charles, La Vern Baker, Joe Turner, Ruth Brown, the Clovers, Aretha Franklin, and the Drifters.[32] Despite his vast achievements in R & B, jazz was Wexler's first love, and it was that mutual interest that brought him and Teddy Reig together.

I MET TEDDY BACK IN THE EARLY 1940s. We used to hang out together. We were all young and into the 52nd Street scene. None of us had any idea of entering the business—we just loved the music. We started out as New Orleans and traditional fans, frequenting Jimmy Ryan's and similar places. Teddy caught onto the new musical trends like bop earlier than most of us.

I was living in Washington Heights at the time, and a bunch of us used to get together to listen to records. We would smoke some grass at these sessions. It was all very innocent— there was no shooting up, no cocaine like there is now. We would all chip in and Teddy would get us a lid because he had all the connections. Teddy was also in charge of rolling. He would roll two for everyone and stash one extra for himself. I have an image of him sitting there, rolling furiously and growling, "Play some Basie," whenever we put on Eddie Condon!

We were all broke, and to pick up some extra cash we would buy up all the old jukebox records and sell them at the Long Island Record Exchange. One side of the disc would be completely beat and the other could still be virgin.

We were all upset when Teddy was arrested in that Ursula Parrott scandal. He went to the can weighing three hundred pounds and came back at one sixty-five. But he was soon right back up there.

Teddy was a real jewel in the rough—a street guy with real character. He didn't suffer fools gladly. I always respected his intransigence, which could also get him in trouble. He wouldn't give up his principles, especially where good music was concerned. I had no business dealings with him, so there was no cause for rancor. I always found him entertaining and fun to be with. I never saw him at work in the studio. It's funny, but record producers never know how other producers work. We just didn't want people around interfering. I always felt that way and I'm sure Teddy did too.

If ever there was a "White Negro," as Norman Mailer termed it, Teddy was one. He married a black woman and disappeared into Harlem. The other two white men I knew who opted for the black life-style were Symphony Sid and Mezz Mezzrow.

A few years ago, I nominated Teddy for the Rock and Roll Hall of Fame. I knew he didn't have much of a chance because the whole thing was too political. At Atlantic we wore two hats: the owners were also the producers. I think that situation existed only at Atlantic and Motown. Teddy, on the other hand, was doing the production work, but he was never part of the owners' crowd and didn't have the connections to be elected. But I felt his R & B work at Savoy was important enough to be recognized.

PAUL WILLIAMS

Paul Williams was born in 1915 in Lewisburg, Tennessee. His family moved to Bowling Green, Ohio, when he was two, and then to Detroit, when he was thirteen. There he studied music at Cass Technical High School and with private teachers. Proficient on many reeds, he played in the leading local bands in Detroit. His recordings for Savoy, and subsequent tours, catapulted him into national prominence with hits like "3530" and "The Hucklebuck." He led his own bands until 1964, when he gave up touring. Turning to studio work, the saxophonist also served as musical director for Lloyd Price and James Brown. Williams has lived in New York since 1960, and in 1968 opened his own booking agency, Paul Williams Entertainment Bureau, which he still operates. Although he rarely plays anymore, in 1986 he made a special appearance at the National Museum of American History in Washington as part of the Smithsonian's symposium on Rhythm and Blues. Williams' association with Teddy Reig began in 1947. Reig produced all of his Savoy recordings, and served as his manager. They remained lifelong friends.

I MET TEDDY THROUGH Savoy Records and Herman Lubinsky. I was working in Detroit at a club and Joe [Von] Battle, who owned a record shop, brought Lubinsky to the club. Lubinsky liked me, so he sent Teddy out to talk to me about recording. He came in and listened and told me he wanted to record me. He didn't want the band, he wanted me. I don't know why—it was a very good band, named for the trumpet player, King Porter. I never wanted to be bothered with a band. I always worked in other people's bands and did very well. Most of the time I was making more money than the bandleader. We set up a date for the recording, and Teddy told me to get my own band together. I used some of the fellows from the band I was

PAUL WILLIAMS
"Exclusive Savoy Recording Artist"

(Courtesy of the Institute of Jazz Studies)

working with. The session took place about a week after we talked.[33]

At that time, I was playing mostly alto and sometimes clarinet. Teddy wanted me to play baritone. I had a baritone, but I very seldom played it. And he had very definite ideas about what I should do. He wanted me to honk. He kept telling me not to play a whole lot of notes. He kept saying, "Honk! Honk! Honk!" I had a pretty rough time pleasing him. I had come up in the swing tradition listening to Jimmie Lunceford, Andy Kirk and Duke Ellington. All the big bands came to Detroit to the Graystone and I didn't miss a one. I was inspired by Benny Carter, Johnny Hodges, Willie Smith, and Earle Warren. And here's this guy telling me to honk! He kept bugging me so much, I almost blew the date. I was so frustrated and upset that I was ready to pack up and leave. Then we did "3530."[34] It was named for the address of Joe [Von] Battle's record shop—3530 Hastings Street. We spent a lot of time there. We'd go in the back and listen to music and watch all the fight films, especially of Joe Louis. We also used to rehearse there. Anyway, I'd had this number in mind, but the band had never played it. I told them just to follow me. It was an instant hit. "The Hucklebuck" was not even heard of at the time, but "3530" was almost as big, and I became known forever as a "honker."

After "3530," everyone started calling me—booking agencies, theaters. I never really wanted to leave Detroit but they kept offering more and more money. Finally, my wife said, "Well, why don't you try it?" I got a wire from Teddy saying he'd gotten us a job at this theater in Baltimore. So I went out. Teddy became my manager with just a handshake. He had connections with the record company and seemed to know what would sell. He was around musicians all the time. He used to hang out and knew everybody. He knew what was happening and loved good music of all kinds.

That first engagement in Baltimore was at the Royal Theater. It was February 20, 1948; I'll never forget the date! Also on the show were Moms Mabley and a great band led by George Hudson. When those cats hit, the crowd went wild

and I said to myself, "What are *we* going to play?" I played
"Hastings Street Bounce" as the first number and it went O.K.
We got a little applause. Then we did a tune called "The
Twister." To me it was just a lot of noise. While I was playing,
the stagehand for some reason kept lowering the mike until
pretty soon it was down to the floor. I just kept blowing into it.
The people went crazy. They thought it was part of the act!
After the first show, the word got around: "Oh man, they got a
saxophone player that'll blow the mike through the stage!" For
the entire week, people were lined up for blocks outside the
box office on both sides of the street. Baltimore became my
town.

Now that it's all over and I've had time to think about what
happened, I think that Leo Parker may have figured in Teddy's
ideas about the baritone and the honking.[35] Leo was one of the
greatest baritone players ever, and he took the country by
storm. He used to end up on that bottom note and shake the
whole house.

"THE HUCKLEBUCK"

It happened during our second or third trip to the Royal Theater. We were always opposite a big band, and this time we were with Lucky Millinder's great band. I was sitting in the audience with a few of the fellows from my band listening to Lucky rehearse. They had a number called "D-Natural Blues." When they began to play it, I looked at one of the cats, and he looked at me. We kept it in mind. After we left Baltimore, our next gig was in Devons, Pennsylvania. The place was packed; it looked like an ocean of people—a wave of dancers. I decided to try the new tune, and the people started doing a dance I had never seen. I went to the edge of the stage and knelt down to watch for a minute or two. I called out, "What is that dance?" "This is 'The Hucklebuck,'" they answered. So that's what we called it. As soon as we got to New York, Teddy recorded us doing it.[36] Lubinsky didn't like it and Teddy bet Herman $1,000 that it would be a hit. Teddy made himself a grand but Lubinsky didn't mind—he made himself a lot of grands!

I always felt the name and the arrangement I had on it made "The Hucklebuck" a hit. It was altogether different from Lucky's. I only got artist's royalties, but you know how that was. To hear Herman tell it, he sold two records! But on the back of "The Hucklebuck" was "Hoppin' John," and that was one of my tunes. So I got something for that—not what I deserved, but something. It was a strange situation because Teddy was managing me and also working for Herman. I didn't know anything about the business on the road. Teddy was a great help to me and he was paid handsomely for it. But then Herman wanted to make a deal with me. He offered either a flat sum or royalties. I said, "What do you think, Teddy?" Teddy shrugs his shoulders and says, "I don't know, man, that's up to you." Suddenly he doesn't know anything! I said, "You're the manager, you can give me some kind of advice!" But Teddy's job depended on Herman. Anyway, I knew Herman wasn't going to give me all my money, so I took a cash settlement. At least I had something, and I would have the artist's royalties coming in anyway. If I was working for someone halfway honest, I could have made some big bucks.

Teddy was alright in the studio. He'd learned a lot of tricks and could make people sound good. He'd put a magazine in the bottom of the bass to get a different sound. Or he'd even put people in the bathroom to get an echo. He learned a lot from the engineers like Jim Syracusa, who did the things in Detroit. He knew the sound he wanted and how to get it. When Teddy recorded Charlie Parker and Miles Davis at Syracusa's studio I was there listening, under the piano. Those cats were playing so much horn! They knew exactly what they were going to play, so Teddy left things pretty much up to them. Teddy was cool till something went wrong. One time at one of my sessions we made a take and one of the engineers couldn't find it. Teddy went crazy. He called this man everything but a tree. I'd never seen a man go stone crazy like that. Eventually they found it or he'd have torn the whole place down.

He got along pretty well with the musicians because he was friends with so many of them. Some thought that he was a pain, but I never saw him have a confrontation with a musician. Teddy was in a bad position. He was in between—working for Herman, and dealing with the musicians.

Teddy was the A & R man for everything I did at Savoy. I don't know why he eventually left Savoy, whether it was a specific incident or not. He and Herman were arguing all the time anyway, so it wouldn't have taken much. Teddy must have figured he was doing so well he didn't need Herman anymore.

ON THE ROAD

When the records took off, we hit the road. Teddy knew what the racial situation was, not just in the South but all over. Even in Detroit, my hometown, you could feel the tension the minute you drove into town. One time we were in Baltimore and Teddy said, "Come on Paul, let's get something to eat." Now, he knew they weren't going to serve me, but he was testing them or some such thing. So we went in and they told him, "We can serve you but we can't serve him." Teddy got all excited and yelled, "Well, why not?" He was sounding things out, but he knew how far he could go or else he'd have gotten both our heads cracked. I tried to cool him out by saying, "I didn't want to eat in there anyway."

He traveled with us quite a bit in the South, but he didn't mess with the people down there too much. We played in all these halls and tobacco barns and the audiences were black. Down there, Teddy was just like a lamb. The people in the audience would be fighting one another. I never played a dance where something didn't break out. I saw some people get real cut up. At a dance, this one cat came in early wearing a zebra-striped coat, as sharp as he could be. After intermission, we hear a disturbance in the back. The people scattered and this same cat comes running toward the band looking for the exit. It looked like they cut every stripe going down! The blood was oozing out of every stripe. He couldn't possibly have lived. Yes, Teddy maintained a low profile.

Most of the time we couldn't stay in hotels, so we slept wherever we could. Once in a while, we did get into white hotels—even in Little Rock. Some people were very polite. You'd go into a store in Jackson, Mississippi, and they would say "yes, sir" and "no sir" to me. And they'd expect you to say that to them. But once you got out of line, you were in trouble. One time, we played a dance in Panama City, Florida—way down there. Afterward, Teddy went to collect the money and this big old sheriff with the wide hat says, "You ain't gettin' no money here tonight." I said, "If he's not going to pay us, let's go." Teddy started to say a little something. I said, "Teddy, let's go! These people don't play here." So Teddy managed to contain himself.

The audiences were black, but a lot of times you had some white people there. They used to have a big rope to divide the races. If someone got out of line, like a white crossing over to the black side, an officer would get up there, stop the music, and say, "Y'all get back over there where you belong!"

What can I say—he was Teddy Reig. He could be the sweetest guy in the world, or he could be the wildest. All in all he tried, but he had an attitude that just couldn't let things go.

It didn't take much to get him going. The first time I met
Teddy, he was cool—very calm and polite. He talked very
nice and said, "Look, I'll make you some money." But soon
after I got to know him, I saw him screaming and hollering at
people. One time we were in Chicago and we were traveling to
Gary. We didn't even have a car. Our transportation then was
buses and the railroad. Just as we got to the bus, the driver
started pulling out. Teddy jumped in front of the bus yelling,
"O.K. Run me over!" He held that bus until we all got on. And
the language he could use! He could do all that stuff and get
away with it.

He was that way right up until the end. In his last years, I
used to go downtown with him because I knew he needed a
little help. If the traffic wasn't moving fast enough, Teddy
would go crazy. I'd be driving and he'd reach over and blow my
horn. I'd have to tell him, "Teddy, don't do that!" Someone
was liable to get out of a car, come back and kill *me*! Another
time he got into it on 14th Street. We went to a health food
store, and some guy tried to take a parking place from him.
Teddy confronted him, saying just about everything you could
possibly say. People came running from all over—the whole
neighborhood turned out. It was tough being with him, raising
all this hell. People like that can get you in trouble. If
something happens, you might as well jump in because they're
going to get you too! He'd go too far with some people, and
when they rebelled, Teddy never could understand it. He'd
call me up and say, "Paul, what's the matter with so-and-so?"

Teddy had two sides and both were extreme. He was
tough, and he was sentimental, especially about the people
and the music he loved. Guys like Benny Carter, Cozy Cole,
Clyde Hart and the others. He loved them to pieces.

In the last few years, the music had changed so much that
Teddy just didn't understand what was happening. It was
another world to him. I used to tell him, "Things are different—you've got to change with it." He would say, "What is
this junk they're playing?" He had a house full of tapes and
records stacked up all over the place. All the stuff that he
loved. I don't know how he found anything. And he'd just stay
in that room and play records. Sometimes he'd call me up just
to play me something over the phone. He stayed close to the

people he loved—Dizzy, Basie. With all his faults and everything, I'd have to say he was a pretty nice guy. He treated me very nice.

JOHNNY SMITH

Guitarist Johnny Smith was born in Birmingham, Alabama, in 1922. He formed his own group, which included tenor saxophonist Stan Getz, while working as a studio musician in New York in the early 1950s. In 1952, he recorded "Moonlight in Vermont" for Teddy Reig's Roost label. It became an instant hit, and was voted Record of the Year in Down Beat. *Over the next decade, the guitarist recorded some fifteen successful albums for Roost. Reig became Smith's manager, and they continued their professional relationship into the late 1960s, and their personal friendship well beyond that. Smith has lived in Colorado Springs since 1958.*[37]

I met Teddy while I was on staff at NBC in New York in 1952. I had organized a quintet which was featured during the course of every program. The show's orchestra was conducted by the musical contractor at NBC, Roy Shields. He asked me to come up with an original every week for the quintet. I think Roy had in mind the Art Van Damme quintet as a model. Stan Getz was in our group along with a piano player named Sanford Gold. Stan certainly didn't need me, but he was trying to get off the road and expressed a desire to do some studio work so he could stay home at least some of the time. We also had Eddie Safranski on bass and Don Lamond on drums. I wrote for the saxophone, piano, and guitar in three-part harmony.

Our pianist, Sanford Gold, was a friend of Teddy's, and he took some of our air checks to him. Teddy had Roost Records then, and he asked me to come see him at their office on 8th Avenue. He told me he was interested in recording a couple of the things of ours. Teddy already had an association with Stan Getz from his earlier recordings with him. So we did a couple of songs. On one side was "Tabu," which was a very fast, flashy piece, and on the other side we decided to do a ballad,

"Moonlight in Vermont." Teddy thought if anything was going to make any noise at all it would be the fast piece. After the session, I took a vacation—I think it was the first I'd ever had! I went down to Florida for about a month. When I got back to New York, people started telling me they'd heard "Moonlight in Vermont" on the radio. I couldn't believe the way it took off. It was one of those weird things. Pretty soon a lot of the jazz disc jockeys across the country started using it as a kind of background while they talked.

Why "Moonlight in Vermont" took off I really don't know. Other guitar players have told me that they were intrigued by my use of closed voicings in harmonizing the melody. On a piano, you can play a closed-voiced chord while keeping your fingers together. But on the guitar, you really have to spread out and, to my knowledge, no other guitar player had used this approach before. I never really thought about it—I just voiced the song the way I heard it and felt it. In fact, everything I did with the group was pretty well planned and just about everything was written out. At the very least, we all knew what harmonies we were going to use. That's one reason I've never been able to refer to myself as a jazz guitarist. I've never been intrigued with jam sessions. Most of my playing to that point had been studio work, performing all kinds of music. I was sort of a musical jack of all trades. To this day, I don't consider myself a jazz player.

Eventually, Stan Getz tired of the studio scene and went back on the road with his own group. Teddy wanted to do some more things with a quintet, so he suggested that we use Paul Quinichette, who was under contract to Decca at the time. They said we could use Paul if I did a recording for them as a tradeoff. Good old Teddy, the hustler, somehow worked it out so that we could use Paul Quinichette's name on the records he did with my group, but they couldn't use my name on theirs. I appeared on the album as "Sir Jonathan Gasser!"[38]

Another weird phenomenon was how my tune "Walk, Don't Run" became a hit. The smaller record companies would always want the artist to include as many original compositions on an album as possible. That would save them paying royalties to the publishers. So, on most of my dates I tried to come up with one or two originals. On this particular date, I came up with this little ditty based on the chord changes to "Softly, as in a Morning Sunrise." It was kind of a contrapuntal arrangement. I didn't have a name for it, so I just called it "Opus." Teddy actually named it "Walk, Don't Run," which got me in trouble because Shorty Rogers had written a jazz piece with the same title. Chet Atkins came to me one night in Birdland and asked if I had any objection if he recorded it. We went into the dressing room, and he played it for me in his style. I told him it was really great and he went ahead and did it. The Ventures heard his record, and they made the rock version which became the big hit.[39] I had very little to do with it—even down to naming it! I don't think the Ventures knew me from Ulysses S. Grant.

My first impression of Teddy Reig was of a hard-nosed businessman. Neither one of us had any high expectations of having a big hit. One thing I will say for him: he never pushed me to change my name! With a name like John Smith, everybody I talked to about becoming a professional musician would advise me to adopt a more distinctive name. It got to the point that I decided to keep it just out of spite!

Teddy and I never had a single agreement in writing. With Teddy, your word was good enough. Teddy acted as my manager. He would be the go-between with the booking agencies, getting me into Birdland or on little tours with my group for a few weeks at a time. He also arranged for me to do some tours with Stan Kenton and Count Basie. Most of these dates were things I wanted to do. Of course, there were times I'd end up working in situations that didn't allow for my first choice of musicians. Many of the top-notch players were working in the studios day and night and you couldn't get them to play for $90 a week in Birdland. Teddy was very good at protecting me from musical situations in which he felt I would be uncomfortable. He often advised me against doing certain dates, and I usually listened to him.

In the studio, Teddy was a total riot. To record for this man was an experience few people could believe. Normally, when you went into a recording studio you were expected to do four songs in three hours. If you didn't, you were in deep trouble, especially with the limited budgets of the smaller companies. So most record dates were very serious and solemn affairs.

Johnny Smith, 1951 *(Courtesy of the Institute of Jazz Studies)*

The people in the control booth would be quiet, the control room most often was blacked out, and you just waited for the voice to say, "Take one!" If you goofed, you'd try again. But with Teddy, it was like a circus! He would come into the control room with a couple of brown paper bags filled with salami and pastrami sandwiches and big bottles of soda. We'd be out there trying to do our best to get an acceptable take, and Teddy would be carrying on in the control room causing a near panic. I don't know how we got anything done! Teddy's big secret of getting the best out of musicians was that he never paid any attention to what was going on in the studio—he never produced anything! Seriously, I always appreciated the fact that Teddy never came back to tell us what we should be doing. He would let the artists have complete freedom. There's nothing more irritating to a musician than having a non-musician tell him what and how to play. Teddy knew enough to keep his nose out of the music.

There were times that Teddy would suggest some things, but he never came on like Mr. Know-It-All. He might come to me and say, "There's a new Broadway show—would you listen to the music?" For example, he sent me up to Boston to hear *The Flower Drum Song* before it opened on Broadway. He asked if I could put together an album based on the musical. It was kind of a disaster because there was so little in it that was adaptable to jazz. But I did the best I could. There were a couple of other instances like that, especially for the last few albums we did together on Verve. Teddy told me it would help him if we did some of the pop things like "Light My Fire" and "Don't Sleep in The Subway." He never asked for help or told me, "You must do this song." So on the few occasions during our association when he did say, "Could you just try and figure out something to do on this piece of shit," I would naturally do what I could for him. You've got to remember that around this time, the late 1950s and early 1960s, the rock and roll bandwagon was creating pressure on Teddy. The whole musical picture was getting very confused, especially as far as jazz was concerned.

By 1957, I was looking to change my life. I wanted a way out of the whole New York music scene. The quality of live music and the business in general was deteriorating. The networks had begun to dissolve their staff orchestras. But what finally prompted me to leave was a personal tragedy: my wife died and I was left with our four-year-old daughter. I was working day and night and had nobody to take care of her. I didn't want to have her raised by sitters. So, in February of 1958 I moved to Colorado Springs; I chose Colorado because we had relatives there. I loaded up my station wagon, and left the city at the height of the rush hour. I drove through the Lincoln Tunnel, and the greatest sight I ever saw in my life was the skyline of Manhattan disappearing in my rearview mirror!

Arthur Godfrey was the only person who tried to dissuade me from leaving. I was doing five daytime shows and the Wednesday night television show with him. He offered to help me in any way, financially or otherwise. When I decided to leave, Teddy was very understanding. He told me, "If that's what you really want to do, that's what you should do!"

I continued to play locally a bit, and in 1959 I began working often in Denver. I also made trips back to New York to work in Birdland and to record. In 1961, I opened a music store which I ran for 26 years until my wife (I had remarried) and I sold it three years ago. I still live in the same house in Colorado Springs that I moved into one week after arriving in Colorado in 1958. I used to do a lot of workshops and seminars at colleges but in recent years, all the schools have had budgetary problems and have had to cut back on visiting "dignitaries." I still play occasionally, but only in situations I find interesting and with people I want to play with.

In the early 1970s, Teddy began having more and more problems with his hip. By 1973, he was in agony. He called me in Colorado and asked if I knew of a good orthopedic surgeon; he said he didn't trust the doctors around New York City. It just so happened that I knew of one of the very best, a friend of mine. That's why Teddy came out here to have his surgery done. They did the operation but, for some reason, Teddy left the hospital prematurely and came to the house. Netta came out to help with him. He developed a staph infection and had to go back into the hospital. When he returned to New Jersey, his hip continued to deteriorate to the point where they couldn't redo the joint replacement. They had to fuse his hip. The doctor who took care of him back East, Dr. Anthony

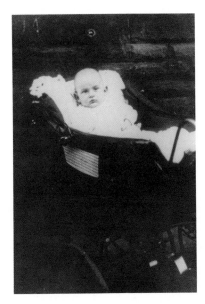

Teddy as a baby. *(Courtesy William Kane)*

With parents. *(Courtesy William Kane)*

A

The White Rose, ca. 1945. *Left to right:* Ben Webster, Teddy, Cozy Cole, Clyde Hart, Charlie Shavers. *(T. Reig Collection)*

Left to right: Mezz Mezzrow, unknown, Thelma Carpenter, unknown, Teddy, Stuff Smith. *(T. Reig Collection)*

B

Back row: Al Hall *(2nd from left)*, Teddy *(2nd from right)*. *Front row:* Nancy Hall *(2nd from left)*, Laurel Watson *(far right)*. *(T. Reig Collection)*.

Back row, men: John Brown, Teddy, Al Hall, Teddy Wilson. Frank Galbreath *(far left in profile)*, Nancy Hall *(in front of Wilson)*. *(T. Reig Collection)*

C

The Trojan Club, Brooklyn, June 23, 1946. Teddy *(foreground)* with *(left to right)* Leonard Gaskin, Winston Craig (emcee), J.J. Johnson, Allen Eager, Max Roach *(hidden)*. *(Courtesy Leonard Gaskin)*

D

In the studio. *(Institute of Jazz Studies)*

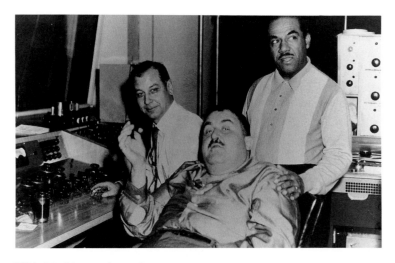

With Machito *(right)*, unknown engineer *(left)*. *(T. Reig Collection)*

With Don Redman, ca. 1960. *(Courtesy Sandra Lovell)*

F

Charlie Parker's funeral, March, 1955. Pallbearers Leonard Feather *(left)* and Teddy. *At far right in doorway:* Charles Mingus. *(Courtesy Leonard Feather)*

Basie band with Frank Sinatra, ca. 1965. Teddy *(far left)*. *Front row left-right:* Al Grey, Eddie Lockjaw Davis, Freddie Greene, unknown, Sonny Payne, Eric Dixon, Charlie Fowlkes, unknown, Sonny Cohn, Harry Edison, Leon Thomas. *Back row left-right:* Quincy Jones, Sinatra, Basie, unknown, Marshall Royal, Bobby Plater. *(Courtesy Sandra Lovell)*

G

Ellington-Basie recording session, July 6, 1961. *Left-right:* Ellington, Teo Macero, Teddy, Basie, Bob Thiele. *(Institute of Jazz Studies)*

Eddie "Lockjaw" Davis and Teddy. *(Chuck Stewart)*

H

With Count Basie. *(T. Reig Collection)*

I

With Count Basie; ladies unidentified. *(Courtesy Sandra Lovell)*.

Barbecue at Count Basie's. *(T. Reig Collection)*

J

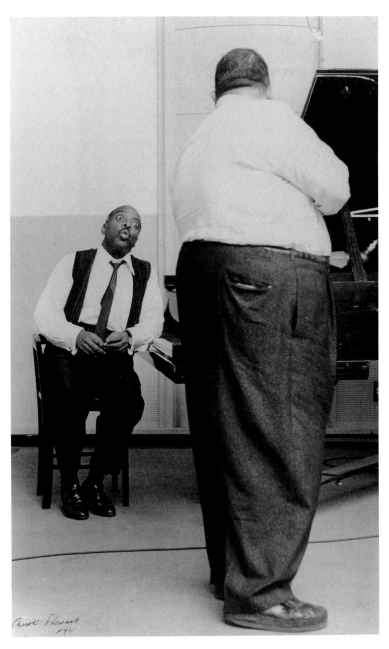

With Count Basie. *(Chuck Stewart)*

Basie session for Impulse Records, March 21, 1962. *Musicians, left-right:* Eric Dixon, Frank Wess, Thad Jones, Basie, Sonny Payne, Freddie Greene, Ed Jones. *(T. Reig Collection)*

With Tony Bennett *(top left)*, Frank Sinatra *(top right)*, Joe Williams.
(Courtesy Sandra Lovell)

M

Teddy and Netta. *(Courtesy Sandra Lovell)*

Teddy and daughter Sandy, graduation from Boston University, May 1977.
(Courtesy Sandra Lovell)

N

Record producers' panel, IAJRC convention, Rochelle Park, NJ, August 20, 1983. *Left-right:* Milt Gabler, Russ Sanjek, Teddy. *(Duncan Schiedt)*

Ed Berger and Teddy, Sweet Basil, NYC, 1982. *(Mitchell Seidel)*

O

(Mitchell Seidel)

P

Santori, was a wonderful person, a dear friend of mine who also played guitar. He did the best he could under the circumstances, but Teddy wasn't the most cooperative patient!

Teddy was really an amazing guy. He had unbelievable energy and was always moving in a hundred different directions. He was tremendously dedicated and hardworking. He loved musicians and had the utmost respect for them. I know for a fact that he literally risked his life to protect musicians from some bad situations. To this day, I know people who just didn't like Teddy. But that has nothing to do with me. He always treated me well, and there's nothing bad I can say about him. But all through the years, I was aware of the other side of the coin.

Teddy was a very volatile person. If he thought somebody was doing something wrong to him or a friend of his, he would blow up. It would be one of the biggest explosions you ever heard; he'd go totally out of control! One time in the late 1950s, Teddy was going to attend a function at the Americana Hotel on 7th Avenue. It was raining and the traffic was really bad. Teddy tried to enter the underground garage at the hotel, but there was a garbage truck blocking the entrance. Teddy got out and asked the driver if he would move up a bit to let everyone pass. The driver snapped back, "Go around the block!" So Teddy got back in the car and drove around the block, which must have taken close to half an hour in that traffic. When he finally made it back, the truck was still sitting there. Once again, Teddy asked the driver to move and again he refused. So Teddy opened the door to the truck, pulled the guy out and threw him down on the pavement. Then he reached into the truck, took the keys and dropped them down a manhole. You can imagine what that did to traffic!

I'm certain I won't live to see anyone else like Teddy Reig, and I'm not sure I'd be ready for it anyway! But he was always wonderful to me; if you were his friend, he'd put down his life for you in a millisecond. That's the way he was.

PHIL KAHL

Phil Kahl was born in 1916, and has been active in the music publishing business. As a partner of Morris Levy, he worked closely with Teddy Reig at Roulette Records and Big Seven Music. He is currently a senior executive with Windswept Pacific Entertainment.

TEDDY DIDN'T PLAY AN INSTRUMENT, but he was a great musician. He had an incredible pair of ears. He loved all the things he was involved in, in the music business, but above all he lived for Basie. He loved Basie and did so much for him. Teddy got him more work, more recording sessions, than anybody else could have. In later years, something happened between them. Not so they didn't talk; things just got a little cool. I never knew why.

Teddy was a character and a pioneer in the business. Nobody understood and appreciated black music better. On the phone, you would think Teddy was black! He loved their music, ate their food, tried to live their life. He was very dedicated to his family and was always concerned about his daughter.

Teddy knew how to have a good time. He used to flash money around. It wasn't unusual for him to carry $5,000 in his shirt pocket! He always had good shit but, as we used to say, he used it on silk sheets. It was done in your home and you knew who you were with. It was never used for exploitation.

I miss the phone calls—even all the yelling! At royalty time, Teddy would start screaming on the phone, "Did the checks come in? Did the checks come in?" He'd even threaten me, "I'm coming to beat the shit out of you!" By the time he arrived at the office, he'd be just like a lamb.

MIKE GOULD

Mike Gould was born in Chicago in 1910 and has spent his life in the music publishing business. He began his career with Irving Mills in 1941, and went on to become Vice President of Capitol Records in charge of publishing. He has also worked for Bourne Music and Liberty Records. His friendship with Teddy Reig dates back to the mid-1940s.

RIGHT FROM THE BEGINNING, jazz has been an essential part of my life. I went to Austin High School near Chicago with Bud Freeman, Davey Tough and Frank Teschemacher. I entered school in 1924. We were together all the time, rehearsing and working. They couldn't read then, but they didn't have to. I was particularly close with Arnie Freeman, Bud's brother, who later became quite an actor. The late 1920s and early 1930s was the most beautiful time in my life. I was around the music constantly and was close to the people who made it.

My introduction into the music business came through Duke Ellington's *Jump For Joy*, which opened in Los Angeles in 1941. I was writing for the magazine *Orchestra World* and was at the theater every night. It was an unbelievable show but it didn't last long because all the people who had put money in it wanted to get it out immediately. Through the show I met Irving Mills, who was so closely tied to Ellington. Mills hired me at practically no salary. I was what was commonly known as a "songplugger." When I joined the service, I got to be known as the only songplugger in the Navy. I used to supply music to 300 Navy bands. In the early 1940s, I was stationed in Washington, D.C. and used to go to New York every weekend. And along came Teddy Reig.

Teddy was into everything—nightclubs, records, managing. We became very close. We used to go to all kinds of restaurants. There was this one Chinese place where, when

Teddy came in, they were off the hook for a week. Then we'd go to another place for lychee nuts. After all that, we'd go to an Italian place he knew and start all over!

Teddy became the all-around record man. If he had to do something Latin, he'd put together a group and it would be as good as it could get. The same thing went for any type of music. One amazing thing about Teddy was how he could blend in with people of any background. In five seconds he could change all his mannerisms. Although he couldn't read music, he had the respect of all the musicians. They believed in him and respected his judgment. When he suggested something, it was invariably right. He had a way of communicating with musicians in their own language. And if things were going right without him, Teddy knew enough to lay out. He also knew the engineers who could get the type of sound he wanted. It was never a job with Teddy—he loved what he was doing.

Whenever Teddy did a session in California, he'd give me a call and I'd drop by. He was always brimming with new ideas. I was at the Sarah Vaughan date where Teddy backed her with only guitar and bass. It was one of those inspired concepts that worked perfectly. He used to have to deal with some pretty crazy situations. And he always kept his sense of humor. I was at another of Sarah's dates where Teddy got involved in a scene with Sarah's then husband, who was not a very nice man. A couple of guns suddenly materialized and Teddy screamed, "They've got guns and I haven't even got a fingernail file!" I remember another incident when Teddy and Phil Kahl were both working at Roulette. I was in Phil's office late one afternoon when Teddy stormed in from a back room. He was mad about something and when Teddy was mad, you could hear him a block away. He screamed at Phil for a while and finally said, "Phil, if they ever make the Jewish version of Porgy and Bess, you'll play Sportin' Life!"

I was in a good position to observe Teddy's relationship with Basie. Basie was very fond of Teddy's wife, Netta, and respected Teddy all the more because of the marriage. Teddy was Basie's right arm—he relied on him for everything. They were extremely close. I was backstage with Basie when he was playing at the Hollywood Bowl. I ran into Stanley Wilson, who was at MCA and he said, "Mike, you know Basie pretty well. Do you think he'd do a theme song for us?" I spent a couple of weeks setting the whole thing up (for which I never saw a penny!) and that was how "M-Squad" came about.

Sure, Teddy was out there hustling all the time and doubletalking people into doing what he wanted. But he also had a heart as big as his body. He helped a lot of people in many ways and never got credit for it. He was one of those tremendous characters of the great years in the music business. There just aren't guys like that anymore. With Teddy it was always happy time.

PETER SPARGO

Pete Spargo was born in 1930, and is the son of Tony Spargo, drummer with the Original Dixieland Jazz Band. He began his professional career in 1947 as a songplugger for the publishing firm of Robbins, Feist and Miller. After doing promotion for Mercury Records, Spargo became a producer for several companies in the 1950s and 1960s. He worked for Roulette in 1965 and 1966, before moving to MGM/Verve, where he remained until 1970. In the 1970s, Spargo engaged in independent production work with Phil Ramone and later joined RCA Records. He currently lives in Fair Lawn, New Jersey, and works for a clinical laboratory. Spargo worked closely with Teddy Reig at Roulette and was instrumental in bringing him to Verve.

I MET TEDDY IN 1965 WHEN I went to work for Roulette Records and their Latin subsidiary, Tico. When I started in January, Teddy was out in California. I'd heard a lot of stories about him—especially about his temper. Sure enough, we got off on the wrong foot. He'd left me some test pressings to check for him. It was an album he'd done with Eddie Palmieri. They sounded fine to me, but Teddy called and started right in screaming, "I don't like that goddamn mix!" By the time he got back to New York he'd calmed down and from then on we got along very well.

When Roulette first started, they had seven million-selling records in a row. Morris Levy had signed Buddy Knox, who did "Party Doll." Then there was Jimmy Bowen and "Stickin' with You." Jimmy, who was Buddy's cousin, was from Texas. He had a friend down there who wanted to record, but Morris turned him down. The friend turned out to be Buddy Holly! But these things happen. The record business is really funny. We used to get demos all the time and we all turned down people who went on to become superstars.

When I was at RCA, we were digging in the files and found out that years earlier they'd turned down a tape of Herb Alpert—singing! It was terrible. There was also an early demo of the Carpenters. That one was an instrumental!

By the time I got there, Roulette had lost a lot of their big jazz names, so Teddy turned to the Spanish stuff. He was running Tico, which was a Latin label which Roulette had acquired. The operation was on the second floor of a building on Broadway and 58th Street. You wouldn't believe what went on up there! Some of the Spanish acts were pretty wild, and they used to bring all their cousins and uncles along. Teddy would be in the middle of this madhouse yelling, "I gotta get out of here!" His assistant was a guy named Pancho Cristal, and he and Teddy fought constantly. Pancho was actually Jewish; his real name was Morris Pelsman. But he spoke Spanish, and acted as the interpreter.

Teddy knew the whole "Spanish network" through his friend Mario Bauza. He brought a lot of artists to the label: Eddie Palmieri, Charlie Palmieri, Joe Cuba, Tito Puente. The Spanish records did very well. Then Morris Levy bought the Paramount Theater and the whole thing went down the drain. We were working under a real "austerity program."

Jazz was Teddy's first love. I was surprised at some of the things he liked. He was crazy about Sonny Rollins, but I don't think he ever recorded him. He once tried to sign John Coltrane for Roulette, but a lot of guys wouldn't go with Morris or Teddy, for that matter.

In 1966, I left Roulette to go to MGM/Verve. I got Teddy a deal with Verve for Johnny Smith. We put Teddy on the 27th floor; he always wanted his own office. Teddy and I also tried to start a Spanish line at MGM, but I never felt it was as successful as it could have been. We did one great album, though: the one with Patato and Totico doing Cuban street songs.[40] Patato was the great conga player, Carlos Valdes. He was a real nice guy but when he recorded with Willie Bobo, he always used to arrive late for the sessions. For his own album, however, he was there half an hour early, wearing a suit and tie!

We did several albums with Willie Bobo and those were good dates. I remember for the first one, *Feelin' So Good*,[41]

Teddy suddenly realized near the end of the date that they hadn't done any of Teddy's own tunes; he wanted a piece of the action as publisher. So he put Bert Keyes, the arranger for the album, into a room and made him write and arrange a tune in half an hour. It turned out to be a hell of a thing called "Sock It to Me." Another song we did with Bobo was "Evil Ways" by Sonny Henry.[42] It started to break big in Chicago but they never pushed it and it died. Then Santana picked it up and cut it a year later, and it became a smash hit. Teddy and Willie Bobo owned the song but Sonny Henry, the composer, sued to get the publishing rights. Teddy and Willie eventually lost the case, which involved a lot of money. Teddy was right morally but wrong legally. He had no papers on it. Teddy wasn't too good with the paperwork. He'd learned from Herman Lubinsky—they did everything on napkins! Of course, Herman was always being sued and he never lost a case. I don't think Teddy really followed through on the Spanish line; his heart wasn't in it at the time. Part of the problem was the turmoil in the company—MGM had five presidents in eleven months!

By this time, Basie had also moved to Verve from Roulette, and Teddy continued to work with him, of course. Teddy and I did the *Basie's Beatle Bag* album together.[43] Teddy became Basie's manager before I met him. From what I gathered, Basie had a big tax problem in the 1950s. Teddy made a few phone calls and bailed him out of a real jam; Teddy had some good connections. Teddy and Basie were really close. One time at Roulette, Teddy was in the office and this English guy comes up to him and says, "Mr. Reig, would you please follow me, sir?" Teddy was a little leery, but he follows the guy downstairs. The guy leads him to a little sports car and asks Teddy to sit in the passenger's seat. Then he asks, "How does it feel?" Teddy says, "O.K." "Are you sure you're comfortable?" "Yeah," Teddy says. "Very good," says the Englishman. "Now Mr. Basie can buy the car; he just wanted to make sure you'd fit."

Basie was a very nice, quiet man. I only saw him flustered once. In 1965, he came up to see Teddy because he'd had a call from the NAACP complaining that there were no whites in his band! Basie was really upset and said he didn't hire guys by color. In the studio, you could always tell when Basie liked an arrangement: he would put his glasses on and really play on it. If he didn't like it, he'd just noodle.

I used to go up to Harlem quite a lot with Teddy, usually to Count Basie's lounge on 135th and Broadway. We'd drive up in Teddy's Mercedes, and as we got closer to Harlem, a funny thing would happen: Teddy's voice would change. He would actually take on a black accent! When he'd walk the streets, he was like the Mayor of Harlem; everybody would yell out, "Hey, Teddy!" Later it changed. In 1982, Redd Foxx was playing up at the Apollo Theater. Redd was very tight with Teddy and sent a limousine with two bodyguards to bring him to the show. It just wasn't possible to walk around up there anymore.

The only time I saw Teddy scared was when we were mixing the Basie Beatles album out in California at the TTG Studios. All of a sudden, Frank Zappa walked in. Teddy took one look at him and ran out of the room saying, "What is that?" Zappa just wanted to hear the band, but he looked so weird that Teddy didn't know what to make of him!

The Basie-Prysock album for Verve[44] was something of a fiasco. There were too many people involved. Instead of letting Teddy do it himself, Mort Nasatir, who was president of MGM/Verve from 1965 to 1968, and Creed Taylor entered the picture. The session was at Rudy Van Gelder's, and everyone in the business heard about it! Rudy is an extremely fussy engineer, even to the point of wearing white gloves to protect against dust. Teddy had trouble with him when he came to scout the place out. Basie had a cup of coffee on the piano, and Van Gelder kept cleaning under it with the white gloves. Mort Nasatir came out to make sure everything went O.K. Rudy had a line drawn on the floor; only he and the producer were allowed past that point. Nasatir, who's president of the company, crossed the line and got yelled at! Creed Taylor tried to eat an apple and also got an argument. Hy Weiss, who was Prysock's manager, lit up a cigar and Van Gelder almost shot him. It was a real comedy! Teddy was ready to kill them all. A few months later, Phil Ramone sent Teddy a pair of white gloves!

Teddy was very good in the studio. He had a real rapport

with the musicians and let the guys play. He wasn't a musician himself, so he never got too involved with the details. But he knew how to get the artists in a good mood so they'd play at their peak. And he always hired good engineers. Sometimes, Teddy's temper would get the better of him. He could blow his stack and actually ruin a session. They tell a story about one of Teddy's dates at RCA studios. Teddy had a big Lincoln Continental at the time. The car was a real lemon, and during the session, Teddy was on the phone trying to get through to the president of Lincoln/Mercury. Teddy yelled and screamed for a while and finally they told him, "If the car's good enough for President Eisenhower, it should be good enough for you!" Well, Teddy slammed the receiver down so hard that he actually smashed the studio board!

Teddy used to do a lot of work at the old Bell Sound studios on 54th Street. The studios were on the fifth floor. The sign in the elevator actually read, "Capacity: seven people—if Teddy's here: two."

Teddy used to fight with all kinds of people. One of his greatest moments came in 1982, when there was a big blackout. Teddy had a lot of fish stored in his freezer. His two-block area in Teaneck was absolutely the last place to have the electricity restored, and Teddy was left with a pile of bad fish. He loaded it all into his car and drove to the Public Service Electric and Gas building in Newark. Somehow, he managed to get into the president's office, where he proceeded to drop fifteen pounds of rotten fish on the man's desk! Teddy demanded compensation and got his money on the spot.

Teddy's temper hurt him in many ways. At MGM he used to give me a hard time, and I was his friend! Later, around 1970 or 1971, he actually went to work for Willard Alexander, but only lasted about three weeks. No one could take his yelling. He was too independent to work for anybody. Teddy hated lawyers, and they really could set him off. In a way, he was very insecure; he always felt people were trying to take advantage of him. That was the nature of the business—all these guys trying to grab whatever they could for themselves. It was almost comical the way the record industry people were so much alike, yet they kept accusing each other of all kinds of things. The truth is that none of them were angels. I finally got out of the business entirely. I just couldn't take it anymore. The guys in charge were no longer interested in music!

I really miss Teddy. He knew how to enjoy life and we had a lot of good times together.

BOB PORTER

Bob Porter is heard regularly on WBGO in Newark. Born in 1940, he has been active as a record producer for over twenty years. He has been associated with such leading labels as Prestige, Milestone, Atlantic, RCA, and Savoy. Among the artists he has produced are Sonny Stitt, Illinois Jacquet, Houston Person, Jimmy McGriff, Hank Crawford, and Gene Ammons. Porter has also contributed to various jazz magazines, as well as assisting Michel Ruppli in the preparation of several detailed label discographies published by Greenwood Press. A two-time Grammy winner, he interviewed Teddy Reig for the award-winning notes to Charlie Parker: The Complete Savoy Studio Sessions.

I FIRST MET TEDDY AT MY RECORD store, Jazz Etc., in North Bergen, New Jersey, in 1974. I was introduced by Roy Roisman, who was a high school friend of Teddy's from Brooklyn. The first thing that struck me about Teddy was that voice; things started to fall from the ceiling! I got to know him pretty well. We used to go to clubs and concerts together. At that time, he didn't have a lot of people he could hang out with anymore. Most of those his own age weren't all that interested in hearing anything. He was already on a cane, but he could still drive. He'd had a hip operation which didn't take, which is why he had that strange walk. I remember one night he wanted to go down to hear Joe Turner at Tramp's. It was a fun evening. We ended up talking and laughing all night with Doc Pomus. Here's four guys at the table: Big Joe Turner, who was on crutches; Doc, who was in a wheelchair; and Teddy with his cane. I remember thinking, "I'm the only one here with legs!"

Because I was in the business as a producer and had done my share of hustling, I went to school on Teddy. There's a lot in this business that he invented! He was interesting, entertaining, educational and frustrating. Teddy could be an enormous pain in the ass, but he could also be very charming and told the funniest stories you ever heard. We would go six months and everything would be cool. Then we'd have a big fight and wouldn't speak for a year.

By 1978, after one of our bouts, we were on good terms again and I interviewed Teddy for the Savoy Charlie Parker boxed set. He thought he was going to pay homage to Bird by talking for half an hour in glowing, mushy terms about how great Bird was. I said, "Teddy, no one wants to hear that. Just say you loved him once and then talk about dealing with him." It was worth doing and he gave us some great stuff. Later, when the notes won a Grammy, Teddy felt that whatever anyone else had done was of no consequence and that *he* was the star and should have gotten the nomination. But that was Teddy—you had to take him as he was. He sure wasn't going to change for you.

I used to pick his brain about Savoy and the sessions he did. What he had to put up with was incredible. For example, Dexter Gordon once got stoned and locked himself in the men's room. Or when they recorded at Harry Smith's studio, which is now Nola on 57th Street above Steinway. There used to be a ledge running outside and the guys used to get high and wander out there. Teddy would have to go out there after them, if you can imagine that sight! He was dealing with a lot of strange people and had to pay plenty of dues just to get those dates done. Especially if Herman Lubinsky was as cheap as Teddy claimed. I'm sure half the kickback schemes that later became standard procedure in the business were invented by Teddy. For example, he used to tell Herman that he'd used seven pieces when there were actually only six. He'd have the trombone player hit a low note and then tell Herman, "That's the baritone."

As an independent A & R guy, he may have been working for Herman, but he was never exclusive to anybody in his whole life. Teddy was like King of 52nd Street in the mid-forties. He would convince Herman to record sessions based on what was happening there. He used to run a place called the Two O'Clock Club. It was a spot somewhere on the Street where musicians could go and leave their stuff—it was always attended. Or they could hang out there during intermissions. He had a million hustles going on all the time, but, you've got to remember, if it wasn't for guys like Teddy, those records probably wouldn't have been made. It's a part of the business people really don't understand. Jazz gets recorded because somebody with an idea approaches somebody with money and says, "Let's do this." Teddy was really good at it.

And once he was in the studio, Teddy knew how to get what he wanted out of these guys. You can hire the greatest musicians in the world, and once the tape starts rolling nothing happens. It's not a good feeling! As far as I'm concerned, he made Don Byas's best records, not to mention Dexter, Bird and a few others. But he was a real master with Basie. The Count Basie band that Teddy produced on Roulette never sounded better anywhere, before or after. Teddy really knew what that band was supposed to sound like and he always got it. It didn't matter where they recorded either. He was involved in everything Basie did, even the sessions he didn't directly produce. He was always Basie's representative. If he wasn't in the booth, then he set it up. For example, the Arthur Prysock session on Verve. He had a big fight with Rudy Van Gelder over that. This was a Verve project and Creed Taylor wanted to record at Van Gelder's studio. So Teddy arrives early, before the band, and Van Gelder asks, "What are you doing here so early?" Teddy tells him, "I want to discuss the setup for the band." Of course, Van Gelder answers him, "What setup? We do it my way!" And he threw him out. Of course, Teddy made a big stink.[45] When Teddy was pissed off, he made sure the entire world knew he was pissed off. And he didn't care who else got pissed off. Teddy and Basie remained absolutely tight right up until the end, well after Teddy was forced to stop working because of his health. I remember going backstage with Teddy at Lincoln Center, and within five minutes he and Basie were deep in conversation, with Teddy telling him all about his latest deals!

Another thing about Teddy's sessions: sometimes he wouldn't use the biggest names in the world but there would be a compatibility about his musicians. He knew what people would get along with each other musically. I mean, Norman Granz records Bird and Diz and has Thelonious Monk and

Buddy Rich in the same rhythm section. You don't find that on Teddy's dates. You choose guys for different reasons. Any record producer who works in this town for any length of time has his regular guys. Their dependability may be more important than the inspiration they bring. For example, a guy I used over and over again—and who was a favorite of Teddy's, incidentally—was George Duvivier. Not only would he be on time and give you exactly what you wanted, but he also knew when things weren't working and how to fix them. You've got to have a guy like that. Clyde Hart used to do it for Teddy, but of course he didn't survive.

One problem with Teddy was that he never felt he got a fair shake from anyone he ever worked for. I wouldn't exactly call it extortion, but somehow he got $2,000 out of Savoy when I was working there in the late 1970s, despite the fact that he himself hadn't worked there since 1951. I'm told he threatened to hold a lawyer outside a window until the guy signed something to release the money! Despite his size, Teddy was always able to fight at any stage of his life. We're not talking about Marquis of Queensberry Rules, however. Once, when he was in his sixties and on a cane, Teddy beat up a postman. The way he described it, Teddy was in one of the malls and this postman bumped him coming out of the door. Some words ensued, and Teddy beat the crap out of him.

Teddy also had very good connections, especially uptown. One time he got a call at two in the morning saying that somebody had stolen a famous actress's coat from Count Basie's club. That would have been a real embarrassment for Basie if it got into the papers. So Teddy got together with a couple of his friends, and somehow they managed to find that coat and get it back to her. They also managed to keep it quiet by putting over the story that it had never left the premises, but had simply been misplaced.

I know some artists felt that Teddy was in it for himself first. Teddy was a hustler and had a lot of different stuff going on at once. Certainly, when he was working for a record company and presenting himself as a personal manager for an artist recording for the same label, well, you're talking about a major conflict of interest. But I'm sure he felt in his own mind that he could serve the needs of everybody.

I was involved in what may have been his last undertaking. In the late 1970s, we started a little label called Natural Organic. Basically, it was for stuff done live and for transcription dates. I'd found the original Black Deuce sessions—the acetates from Carnegie Hall in 1947 with Bird and Dizzy and Ella. Teddy claimed they were his and that Herman had kept them from him all those years. There's no question in my mind that Black Deuce was a Savoy operation, but that Teddy was instrumental in getting it off the ground. The stuff ended up on Birdland ten-inch LPs, later on Roost, and then on Roulette. It all went through Teddy, but he never had access to the original discs. So we put that out, along with some Red Norvo transcriptions with Tal Farlow and Charles Mingus. I just let it go after a while. I was supposed to have a piece of the company and there was a friend of Teddy's who'd just gotten out of jail who was supposed to have another piece. Teddy always used to say, "Look, when I go to dinner, everybody eats!" What he neglected to add was that he had a very big appetite, and he always ate first!

Teddy was larger than life. Now that he's gone, you look back and remember the funny bits. But he could be a son-of-a-bitch. It was done his way or no way. But he was operating in different times. How he accomplished what he did, given those conditions, was a miracle. I don't care who says he got screwed out of this, hustled out of that, shafted, dumped on, or whatever. Ultimately, what's important is the music. Just listen to the records. They're Teddy's legacy.

SANDRA REIG LOVELL

Sandy Lovell is Teddy Reig's daughter. She is a graduate of Boston University with a major in psychology and lives in Scotch Plains, New Jersey, with her husband, Ellsworth. Ellsworth also contributed some reminiscences; to identify the speaker, Sandy's remarks are prefaced by "SL," Ellsworth's by "EL."

SL: I was born in Bermuda in 1955 and was adopted by my parents when I was five years old. My mom came down and the adoption took place there. She brought me home to St. Albans, in Queens. We lived on Adelaide Lane, right across the street from Count Basie and around the corner from Milt Hinton. One of the first things I remember is swimming in Uncle Basie's pool. My father was a big man and had these enormous swim trunks. He used to dive in and I would put my arms around his neck. That's how I learned how to swim.

Shortly after, we moved to Teaneck, New Jersey. I remember going to kindergarten in St. Albans and first grade in Teaneck. My father was great to a kid because he could never say no! I had everything I could ever want; nothing was too good for his little girl. He also never laid a hand on me—he left all of that to my mother. She always used to say he was too easy. He loved to take me on long drives—usually on the spur of the moment—around New Jersey or into New York. He was on the road a lot himself because of his work. After he had his hip operation, and moved his business from New York, he was home a lot more. He had the operation in Colorado about the time I was entering college.

It's funny, but for years I never knew exactly what he did, although I knew he was in the music business. If someone asked me, I would say he was an A & R man, but I couldn't tell you what *that* was! I knew he ran several companies, and we had a business phone in the house under Forshay Music. He also had a lot of checkbooks with all these different music companies on them. Boxes of records would arrive at the house and whenever people came over my father would say, "Here, listen to this. I'll make you one." If there was a particular tune he liked, all the neighbors knew it because of the volume. He would sit in his huge green chair and thump his foot in time to the music. His stomach would also shake in time!

As I got older, he started taking me to recording sessions. I remember one in particular. My father was doing a date in California with Sarah Vaughan and we all went out there. They let me stay inside the studio while they were recording. I used to wear silver bangles at the time, and when they played it back all you could hear was this clanking sound! Needless to say, they threw me out. There were other sessions—Quincy Jones, Ray Charles, Duke Ellington—but most of the time the music went over my head.

I also spent a lot of time backstage with the Basie band at concerts and shows. Freddie Greene was my buddy; we used to play cards all the time. In fact, one of the albums my father produced with Basie was made because of me. I was always falling asleep at the sessions, so they decided to find something that would appeal to young people of my generation. They came up with *Basie's in the Bag*, and there's even a bit in the liner notes about me.[46] That was my only contribution to the music world!

I was brought up in a crazy household. My mother was black and Baptist, my father was white and Jewish, my mother's mother was Catholic. I used to attend one church with my mother, another with my grandmother, and go to synagogue with my father.

My father's mother, whom I never met, had been very much opposed to my parents' marriage and she alienated my father's family from him. She used to call the house sometimes and if my mother or I answered, she would just say, "May I speak to Teddy." She was almost nasty about it. I remember my father getting on the phone and telling her that if she couldn't be polite, then not to call at all. He hardly ever went to see her. When she got sick, my mother browbeat him into visiting her. And when she died, my mother forced him to go to her funeral. My father was very bitter because his mother never accepted us and turned his whole family away.

One interesting thing happened after my father's mother died. Her sister—my father's aunt—came to visit my father when he was in the hospital. That was the first time she and my mother ever met. She was very pleasant and gave my mother a check for $1,000 saying, "This is the wedding present I should have given you years ago." Once his mother died, my father's family did sort of come back. After my father died, I found out that he and his Uncle Bill [Kane] in Nevada had gotten pretty close. Although we've never met, we still exchange Christmas cards. But my father would never ask his family for anything, even when he could have used the help. There was no problem with my mother's family; they accepted my father.

Because I'm black and my father was white, people used to raise their eyebrows. Once when I was a kid, we were shopping in Saks and I drifted away from him. I started yelling, "Daddy! Daddy!" When he came running, everybody turned to look. I went to private school and on parents' night there was quite a stir when my parents arrived. But it was mostly surprise. I don't remember much negative reaction; after all, my father was pretty imposing!

"Explosive" is the best word to describe my parents' relationship. As a child, I couldn't understand why they were always battling. If you can't get along, why stay together? I used to think, "These people can't really love each other." They'd even separated a couple of times. My mother had moved to California and talked about divorcing him. But there was some kind of bond there that was unshakable. My mother was the only one who could tell my father what to do and actually have some effect. She made him do a lot of the "right" things. She had become his anchor.

My father's public image was the same one he conveyed at home. I can chuckle about it now, but he used to rant and rave like a lunatic. I heard every swear word there was, and quite a few he made up on the spur of the moment. We had a lot of fun together, but we also had some terrible yelling matches. At first, I was intimidated and would never yell back because his voice just overwhelmed me. But, over the years, I began to realize that a lot of it was hot air, and I'd just yell right back.

One reason he was so loud was that he was a little deaf, although he would never acknowledge it. You really had to scream for him to hear you.

As I got older, I began to understand his personality more. He would say some devastating things that he didn't really mean. He would regret what he said but he would never apologize. Instead, he would give flowers or cookies.

EL: I know he didn't intend to hurt people. When Sandy and I first met, my grandfather had recently passed away and left me his watch. One evening we were sitting at the kitchen table and Teddy looked at the watch and said, "What's that piece of shit you got there?" He must have seen the expression on my face because he took a solid gold watch off his wrist and gave it to me. A couple of days later, he came and explained that he hadn't meant to hurt me.

SL: Despite the blow-ups, my father basically loved people—all kinds of people. He was a great storyteller, and was always the center of attraction, no matter what the group. His real name was Theodore Samuel Reig, but he was Teddy to everyone. Even today, everybody I run into who knew my father has a story about him. And he seemed to know everybody— people in all walks of life, from gangsters to bank presidents. He was the same around everyone. He never dealt with the shadier characters at home, but I used to go with him to some really strange places in the city and he'd pull over and say, "Stay in the car, I'll be back in a minute." We never had to wait in line for a club or a show. If my father wanted to get tickets, he never called Ticketron; he called the owner or the producer!

EL: He took me to places in lower Manhattan I'd never dreamed of. He pointed out where every gangster used to live and who owned what building. We went into the basements of all the restaurants, with the food hanging all around us. He showed me where he used to hang out. This was only a few months before he died and, wherever we went, everyone still knew him. You can imagine what it was like in his prime. I'd just met him and was trying to make a good impression because I wanted to marry his daughter. I'd heard all about his being a raving maniac! That day I really got an insight into Teddy. And that night we sat and talked for hours. He must have known he was near the end, because he kept saying, "I'm on the way out."

On another one of his wild tours, we passed by Katz's delicatessen and he asked if I wanted a hot dog. We went in and he ordered whatever he wanted—no charge. I asked him how he could do that and he explained that one night he was out with Frank Sinatra and they needed some place to sit down and go over some contracts. So they went to Katz's and the manager let them use his office. The guy was so overwhelmed at having Sinatra there that he told Teddy, "Anytime you want anything just help yourself!"

SL: He saw through color and nationality—they didn't mean much to him. He fit right in because he genuinely liked people. Also, because he had been ostracized by his own family, he refused to let those attitudes into his own life. As a white man in Harlem, my father went everywhere. He was never afraid because everyone knew him by name and he was welcome. The same thing happened in the Spanish community. He knew all the places to go and, again, because of the music, he was drawn to the culture. He also loved to go to Chinatown, and everyone knew him there, too. On the spur of the moment, he would take all of us to his favorite restaurant—Young Luck. All the waiters would surround him and he would order for everyone. He never wanted a menu. He would tell them, "Bring me what the real Chinese people eat!"

Outside of music, he didn't have too many interests. When I was a kid, I remember him reading all the time and as I got older, we would swap books. He would read everything: novels, four daily newspapers, anything. When he got sick, he used to read all the medical books and then tell the doctor what to prescribe.

His other main interest was food! At one time he had a fifty-inch waist. A friend and I took a pair of his pants and we each stood comfortably in one of the legs! He was supposed to be watching his weight but my friends would always catch him eating. They'd tell me, "I saw your father at Friendly's," or "I saw your father at the ice cream place." Then he'd come home and announce that he was starving and hadn't had a bite to eat all day!

Once he brought home a piece of pastrami from some special place in New York. He gave careful instructions on how to steam it and then left on some errand. My mother and I were supposed to be watching it, but we both fell asleep. When I woke up, the house was full of smoke, the pot had burned, and the pastrami was charred. Now I'm in a real panic. My father would have killed us for ruining his pastrami! So we opened all the windows and sprayed air freshener. Then I raced over to the nearest delicatessen and tried to find a piece that was roughly the same size and shape. We heated it up and he never knew the difference. He swore up and down that we were eating the best pastrami in the world, and that you couldn't find it anywhere else!

There were some lean years after he had to stop working. He was getting a disability check, and it was hard for him to adjust to just having enough for the basics. He had been living pretty high. His pockets were always full of money and he used to drive a Mercedes, although as soon as I got my license he traded it in for a Chevy! He used to hide money all over the place—in his car, in album covers. One time my mother had me cleaning up around the back steps when I came across this paper bag. I opened it up and there were bugs crawling around, so I threw it in the air and money started flying out! There was over $1,000. I don't know how long it had been there, but it was turning yellow. Along with it there was a deposit slip which my father had written out. My father never told my mother he'd lost it, and we never told him we'd found it!

He also loved fine clothes, and used to be a real natty dresser. He had all his clothes made from the finest material. When he was no longer able to work he was forced to be more budget conscious. It was strange seeing him shopping at Syms after he'd been wearing custom-made cashmere coats.

My father used to drive us all over. Unfortunately, he was the world's worst driver. I used to just close my eyes and pray. He would constantly curse out everyone on the road. They were always wrong, he was always right! He would cut between two lanes without signaling. If the speed limit was sixty, he'd do forty in the fast lane. He had some accidents that you couldn't figure out at all. Once he even came back with the roof of his car all dented. He thought nothing of hopping out and assaulting another car with his cane!

He loved living his life in the time in which he grew up; it was perfect for him. But time just moved past him and he couldn't accept it. His manner alienated a lot of people, but he knew how to get things done. He never wanted to talk to the middle guy; he always went straight to the top. But the world had changed. The people running the music industry were now accountants and lawyers, not people like my father who could hear the music and know it was right. He couldn't relate to them and he became very disgruntled at the "three-piece suits."

When my mother got cancer, he was totally destroyed. She had never been ill in her life and my father had been in such poor health that he never thought he would outlive her. The original prognosis was six months, but she lived longer than that. She was a very strong person and when she found out, she started putting her affairs in order. She died on April 23, 1983. After her death, my father became reclusive. He wouldn't answer the phone or the door sometimes. It wasn't that people stopped coming; he just wouldn't let them into his life anymore.

He didn't like it when I moved to Bermuda. He would have wanted me close by so he could keep an eye on me. I don't think he ever realized I was grown until I moved. He may have felt threatened by the fact that I had moved back to my place of birth; he was afraid that I might be pulling away from him. I think he eventually came to realize that, wherever I was, I had only one father and one mother. He himself loved Bermuda, and used to go there often even before I moved there. In fact, he was cremated, and in his will he asked that his ashes be scattered in Shelly Bay, where he used to go swimming. My husband and a friend got a boat and did it.

He was terrific in his own way. I learned a lot about life from him. I always used to say, "I'm not like my father," but as I get older, I know I have some of his mannerisms. I don't yell and scream, but I learned not to take any crap from anybody. I

Teddy Reig *(E. Berger)*

have his skepticism. I have more patience than he did, but then
he didn't have any! He was my father and he was unique.

Teddy Reig's Productions:
A Selected Discography

INTRODUCTION

THIS DISCOGRAPHY IS A BASIC guide to recordings produced by Teddy Reig. Various non-Savoy 78 rpm sessions of the 1940s are listed first. The sections which follow are devoted to Reig's major record company associations: Savoy, Roost, and Roulette. Within each label, the arrangement is alphabetical by artist; under each artist, sessions or albums appear in chronological order. Reig's work with Count Basie, regardless of label, has been listed separately, as have his Latin productions. A final, miscellaneous section contains LPs which do not fit into the aforementioned categories. Personnel is given for 78 rpm sessions, but not for LP dates. The format varies slightly from section to section:

SAVOY

Because the Savoy period is well documented in Ruppli's *The Savoy Label: A Discography*, original 78 rpm issue numbers have not been included. Reissues are noted below each session; no attempt has been made to list all issues, only the most recent or readily available. Some sessions (primarily those which have not been included in the Savoy reissue series) are represented by a date alone. Full information is available in Ruppli.

ROOST

Format is similar to that of Savoy, but original 78 issue numbers follow the song titles.

LATIN

LPs are arranged by artist and include all labels. It was impossible to establish dates for Reig's Tico albums; most were probably recorded between 1961 and 1966.

FORMAT FOR LP LISTINGS

Date of recording, title (in italics), and original issue number are supplied. An asterisk following the issue number means that the compiler has seen the LP and that Reig is given production credit on the sleeve. Recent reissues are indicated, including CDs, in many cases. Unless otherwise noted, reissue numbers pertain to the same label as the original recording. As a rule, only original sessions produced by Teddy Reig are included; reissue LPs and anthologies compiled by Reig are not listed.

Apart from the sleeve credits and, in the case of some 78s, label credits, various sources were used to establish the fact that Reig produced a given session. Teddy himself identified many of his productions, either from memory or by looking through relevant discographies. In the case of Savoy recordings, Bob Porter, who has done detailed research on the label, was able to supply information. Jack Hooke, Reig's partner at Roost, supplied similar details for that label. Hooke recalled that Reig was instrumental in setting up most of the Roost sessions, and that they shared production responsibilities. Although Teddy was not actually present at all Roost dates, particularly in later years when his duties on the road increased, he continued to play an essential role in organizing them. Hooke was able to identify many of these sessions which Teddy did not supervise directly, and they have been excluded from the discography. Pete Spargo, who worked with Teddy at Roulette and Verve, provided information about Teddy's activities for those labels, as well as for Roulette's Latin subsidiary, Tico. In some cases, musicians have been consulted to verify Reig's participation.

EARLY NON-SAVOY SESSIONS

FIRST SESSION:

Clyde Hart's All Stars/Trummy Young's All Stars
January 1945
  Dizzy Gillespie, Trummy Young, Charlie Parker, Don Byas,
  Clyde Hart, Mike Bryan, Al Hall, Specs Powell, Rubberlegs
  Williams

  What's the Matter Now? (Continental C6013)
  I Want Every Bit of It (Continental C6020)
  That's the Blues (C6013)
  4-F Blues (C6020)
  Dream of You (C6060)
  Seventh Avenue (C6005)
  Sorta Kinda (C6005)
  Ooh, Ooh, My, My, Ooh, Ooh (C6060)

  First four titles on Onyx 224, *Charlie Parker: First Recordings.* All
  titles on Spotlite SPJ-150D, *Every Bit of It.*

Erroll Garner
September 9, 1949
  Leonard Gaskin, Charlie Smith

  Scatter-Brain (3 Deuces 508/Roost 609)
  Through a Long and Sleepless Night (3 Deuces 505)
  Again (3 Deuces 506/Roost 610)
  What Is This Thing Called Love? (3 Deuces 505/Roost 606)

  Last three titles on Mercury SR-60662, Erroll Garner: *Misty.*
  First title on Mercury 842-889-1, *Best of Garner.*

Erroll Garner/Johnny Hartman
August 23, 1949
  Leonard Gaskin, Charlie Smith

  Remember/September in the Rain (Mercury 5378)

Easy to Remember/Home (Mercury 8152)

Frankie Socolow
May 2, 1945
  Freddy Webster, Bud Powell, Leonard Gaskin, Irv Kluger

  The Man I Love/Reverse the Charges (Duke 112)
  Blue Fantasy/September in the Rain (Duke 115)

SAVOY

Emmett Berry
January 8, 1946
  Illinois Jacquet, Bill Doggett, Freddie Greene, John Simmons, Shadow Wilson

  Savoy Blip/Illinois Goes to Chicago/Doggin' with Doggett/ Minor Romp/Berry's Blues

  Four titles on SJL-2220, *The Tenor Sax Album*; alternates on SJL-2224, *The Changing Face of Harlem, v. 2.*

Tiny Bradshaw
March 11, 1947

Pete Brown
February 20, 1945
March 6, 1945

Milt Buckner (The Beale Street Gang)
October 28, 1946
December 8, 1947
July 11, 1948
April 5, 1951

Don Byas
November 26, 1945
  Benny Harris, Jimmy Jones, John Levy, Fred Radcliffe

  Candy/How High the Moon/Don By/Byas-a-Drink

  All on SJL-2213, Don Byas: *Savoy Jam Party.*

May 17, 1946
  Ted Brannon, Franklin Skeete, Fred Radcliffe

I Don't Know Why/London Donnie/Old Folks/Cherokee/
September in the Rain

All on SJL-2213, Don Byas: *Savoy Jam Party.*

August 21, 1946
Sanford Gold, Leonard Gaskin, Max Roach

Living My Life for You/To Each His Own/They Say It's Wonder-
ful/Cynthia's In Love/September Song/St. Louis Blues/ I Found a
New Baby/Marie

All on SJL-2213, Don Byas: *Savoy Jam Party.*

Serge Chaloff
March 5, 1947
Red Rodney, Earl Swope, George Wallington, Curly Russell,
Tiny Kahn

Pumpernickel/Gabardine and Serge/Serge's Urge/A Bar a
Second

All titles, including alternates, on SJL-2210, *Brothers and Other
Mothers.*

Earl Coleman
June 23, 1948

Cousin Joe (Pleasant Joseph)
February 13, 1946
Leonard Hawkins, Pete Brown, Ray Abrams, Kenny Watts, Jim-
my Shirley, Leonard Gaskin, Arthur Herbert

Weddin' Day Blues/Desperate G.I. Blues/You Got It Comin' to
You

All on SJL-2224, *The Changing Face of Harlem, v. 2.*

May 21, 1947

Tadd Dameron
October 28, 1947
Fats Navarro, Ernie Henry, Curly Russell, Kenny Clarke, Kay Penton

A Bebop Carol/The Tadd Walk/Gone with the Wind/That Someone Must Be You

All titles on SJL-2216, Fats Navarro: *Fat Girl.*

Eddie "Lockjaw" Davis
December 18, 1946
Fats Navarro, Al Haig, Huey Long, Gene Ramey, Denzil Best

Calling Dr. Jazz/Fracture/Hollerin' and Screamin'/Stealin' Trash

All on SJL-2216, Fats Navarro: *Fat Girl.*

December 20, 1946
as above

Just a Mystery/Red Pepper/Spinal/Maternity

Reissue as above.

Lem Davis
March 6, 1946
Neal Hefti, Hal Singer, Sanford Gold, John Simmons, Denzil Best

Theme on the Beam/Solace/Chitlin Strut/Daily Double

All on SJL-2224, *The Changing Face of Harlem, v. 2.*

May 10, 1946
Courtney Williams, Vic Dickenson, Sanford Gold, Al Hall, Denzil Best

I Don't Believe/I Never Knew/Lovely You/ G-U-M-P-E-Y

All on SJL-2224, *The Changing Face of Harlem, v. 2.*

Miles Davis
August 14, 1947
Charlie Parker, John Lewis, Nelson Boyd, Max Roach

Milestones/Little Willie Leaps/Half Nelson/Sippin' at Bells

Master takes on SJL-2201, Charlie Parker: *Bird—The Master Takes*. Complete session, including alternates, on SJL-5500, Charlie Parker: *The Complete Savoy Studio Sessions* and on 2DS-5500, a set of three compact discs. Complete session, including newly discovered fragments on Savoy SJL-1196, Miles Davis: *First Miles*.

Allen Eager
March 22, 1946
    Ed Finckel, Bob Carter, Max Roach

    Rampage/Vot's Dot/Bo By Hatch/Symphony Sid's Idea

    All on SJL-2210, *Brothers and Other Mothers*.

July 15, 1947
    Terry Gibbs, Duke Jordan, Curly Russell, Max Roach

    All Night, All Frantic/Donald Jay/Meeskite/And That's for Sure

    Reissue as above.

November 6, 1947
    Doug Mettome, George Wallington, Leonard Gaskin, Stan Levey

    Nightmare Allen/Churchmouse/Jane's Bounce/Unmeditated

    All titles, including alternates, on SJL-2236, *Brothers and Other Mothers, v. 2*.

Redd Foxx
September 30, 1946
    Johnny Swan, Pazuza Simon, Kenny Watts, Les Millington, Arthur Herbert

    Let's Wiggle a Little Boogie/Lucky Guy/Fine Jelly Blues/ Redd Foxx Blues/Shame on You

    All on SJL-1181, Redd Foxx/Dusty Fletcher: *Open the Door Richard*.

Erroll Garner
September 25, 1945
  John Levy, George De Hart

  Laura/Stardust/Somebody Loves Me/Indiana

  All on SJL-2207, *Erroll Garner—The Elf.*

Stan Getz
July 31, 1946
  Hank Jones, Curly Russell, Max Roach

  Opus De Bop/And the Angels Swing/Running Water/Don't
  Worry 'bout Me

  All on SJL-1105, Stan Getz: *Opus De Bop.*

May 2, 1949
  Earl Swope, Zoot Sims, Al Cohn, Duke Jordan, Jimmy Raney,
  Mert Oliver, Charlie Perry

  Stan Gets Along/Stan's Mood/Slow/Fast

  Master takes on SJL-1105; alternates on SJL-2210, *Brothers and
  Other Mothers.*

Sanford Gold
May 8, 1946

Dexter Gordon
October 30, 1945
  Sadik Hakim, Gene Ramey, Ed Nicholson

  Blow Mister Dexter/Dexter's Deck/Dexter's Cuttin' Out/
  Dexter's Minor Mad

  All on SJL-2211, Dexter Gordon: *Long Tall Dexter.*

January 29, 1946
  Leonard Hawkins, Bud Powell, Curly Russell, Max Roach

  Long Tall Dexter/Dexter Rides Again/I Can't Escape from You
  Dexter Digs In

  All titles, including alternates, on SJL-2211.

December 11, 1947
    Leo Parker, Tadd Dameron, Curly Russell, Art Blakey

    Settin' the Pace 1 & 2/So Easy/Dexter's Riff

    All titles, including alternates, on SJL-2211.

December 22, 1947
    Fats Navarro, Tadd Dameron, Nelson Boyd, Art Mardigan

    Dexter's Mood/Dextrose/Index/Dextivity

    All on SJL-2211.

Milt Jackson
February 23, 1949
    Bill Massey, Julius Watkins, Billy Mitchell, Walter Bishop, Nelson Boyd, Roy Haynes

    Hearing Bells/Junior/Bluesology/Bubu

Illinois Jacquet
January 7, 1946
    Emmett Berry, Bill Doggett, Freddie Greene, John Simmons, Shadow Wilson

    Don't Blame Me/Jumpin' Jacquet/Blues Mood/Jacquet in the Box

    All on SJL-2220, *The Tenor Sax Album*; alternates of first and last titles on SJL-2224, *The Changing Face of Harlem, v. 2.*

J. J. Johnson
June 26, 1946
    Cecil Payne, Bud Powell, Leonard Gaskin, Max Roach

    Jay Bird/Coppin' the Bop/Jay Jay/Mad Be-Bop

    All titles, including alternates, on SJL-2232, J. J. Johnson: *Mad Be-Bop.*

December 24, 1947
    Leo Parker, Hank Jones, Al Lucas, Shadow Wilson

    Boneology/Down Vernon's Alley/Yesterdays/Riffette

All on SJL-2232.

May 11, 1949
Sonny Rollins, John Lewis, Gene Ramey, Shadow Wilson

Audobahn/Don't Blame Me/Goof Square/Bee Jay

All titles, including alternates on SJL-2232.

Kenny Kersey
July 30, 1946

Morris Lane
January 24, 1947
June 30, 1948

Milt Larkin
January 12, 1949

Brownie McGhee
October 20, 1947
December 19, 1947
1948 (several sessions)
March 22, 1949

> Complete October 20, 1947, Spring 1948, December 20, 1948, and March 22, 1949, sessions on Savoy SJL-1204, Brownie McGhee: *Jumpin' The Blues*.

Billy Moore and His Jumping String Octet
April 20, 1945

Brew Moore
October 22, 1948
Gene Di Novi, Jimmy Johnson, Stan Levey

Brew Blew/Blue Brew/No More Brew/More Brew

All titles, including alternates, on SJL-2210, *Brothers and Other Mothers*.

May 20, 1949
    Jerry Lloyd, Kai Winding, Gerry Mulligan, George Wallington, Curly Russell, Roy Haynes

    Mud Bug/Gold Rush/Lestorian Mode/Kai's Kid

    All titles, including alternates, on SJL-2236, *Brothers and Other Mothers, v. 2.*

Wild Bill Moore
November 21, 1947
December 18, 1947

Vido Musso
February 25, 1946
    Kai Winding, Gene Roland, Boots Mussulli, Marty Napoleon, Eddie Safranski, Denzil Best

    Moose in a Caboose/Moose on the Loose/My Jo-Ann/Vido in a Jam

    All on MG12074, *Loaded.*

Fats Navarro
January 29, 1947
    Tadd Dameron, Gene Ramey, Denzil Best

    Fat Girl/Ice Freezes Red/Eb Pob/Goin' to Minton's

    All on SJL-2216, Fats Navarro: *Fat Girl.*

December 5, 1947
    Charlie Rouse, Tadd Dameron, Nelson Boyd, Art Blakey

    Nostalgia/Barry's Bop/Bebop Romp/Fat Blows

    All titles, including alternates, on SJL-2216.

Charlie Parker
November 26, 1945
    Miles Davis, Dizzy Gillespie, Curly Russell, Max Roach, Sadik Hakim

Warming Up a Riff/Billie's Bounce/Now's the Time/Thriving from a Riff/Koko/Meandering

Master takes on SJL-2201, Charlie Parker: *Bird—The Master Takes*. Complete session, including alternates, on SJL-5500, Charlie Parker: *The Complete Savoy Studio Sessions* and on 2DS-5500, a set of three compact discs.

May 8, 1947
Miles Davis, Bud Powell, Tommy Potter, Max Roach

Donna Lee/Chasing the Bird/Cheryl/Buzzy

Reissues as for previous session.

December 21, 1947
Miles Davis, Duke Jordan, Tommy Potter, Max Roach

Another Hair Do/Bluebird/Klaunstance/Bird Gets the Worm

Reissues as for previous session.

September 18, 1948
Miles Davis, John Lewis, Curly Russell, Max Roach

Barbados/Ah-leu-cha/Constellation/Parker's Mood

Reissues as for previous session.

September 24, 1948
as above

Perhaps/Marmaduke/Steeplechase/Merry-Go-Round

Reissues as for previous session.

NOTE: A selection of Parker's Savoy work appears on SJL-1208, Charlie Parker: *Original Bird—The Best of Bird on Savoy*.

Leo Parker
October 4, 1947
Howard McGhee, Gene Ammons, Junior Mance, Gene Wright, Charles Williams

El Sino/Ineta/Wild Leo/Leapin'Leo

All on SJL-1103, Gene Ammons: *Red Top*.

December 19, 1947
  Joe Newman, J. J. Johnson, Dexter Gordon, Hank Jones, Curly
  Russell, Shadow Wilson

  Wee Dot/Solitude/The Lion Roars/Mad Lad Boogie

  Master takes and alternates of first and third titles on SJL-2211,
  Dexter Gordon: *Long Tall Dexter* and SJL-2225, *The Bebop Boys*.

March 23, 1948
  Joe Newman, Charlie Rouse, Sir Charles Thompson, Al Lucas,
  Jack "The Bear" Parker

  On the House/Dinky/Senor Leo/Chase 'n Lion/Leo's Bells/
  Sweet Talkin' Leo/Swinging for Love/The New Look

  Five titles on SJL-2225.

Pleasant Joseph (*see* **Cousin Joe**)

Doc Pomus
November 6, 1947

Ike Quebec
August 7, 1945
  Johnny Guarnieri, Bill De Arango, Milt Hinton, J. C. Heard

  Girl of My Dreams/Jim Dawgs/Scufflin'/I.Q. Blues

  All on SJL-2220, *The Tenor Sax Album*.

Teddy Reig
January 22, 1947
  Kai Winding, Allen Eager, Marty Napoleon, Eddie Safranski,
  Shelly Manne

  O-Go-Mo/Mr. Dues/Oh, Kai/Saxon

  All on SJL-2236, *Brothers and Other Mothers, v. 2*.

  NOTE: For contractual reasons this session issued as "Teddy
  Reig's All Stars."

Eddie Safranski
February 26, 1946

George Shearing
February 3, 1947
    Gene Ramey, Denzil Best

    So Rare/Have You Met Miss Jones/George's Boogie

    First two titles on SJL-1117, George Shearing: *So Rare*.

February 1947
    Gene Ramey, Denzil Best

    Buccaneer's Bounce/When Darkness Falls

    Both on SJL-1117.

December 23, 1947
    Curly Russell, Cozy Cole

    Bop's Your Uncle/Sweet and Lovely/Cozy's Bop/Sophisticated
    Lady

    All on SJL-1117.

Hal Singer
June 1948
    Milt Larkin, Wynton Kelly, Franklin Skeete, Heywood Jackson

    Swanee River/Jumpin' in Jack's House/Plug for Cliff/Corn Bread

    First and third titles on SJL-2234, *The Roots of Rock 'n' Roll, v. 6*;
    last title on SJL-2221, *The Roots of Rock 'n' Roll* and SJL-1147, Hal
    Singer: *Rent Party*.

September 10, 1948
    Rent Party/Singer Song/Rice and Red Beans/Swing Shift

    All on SJL-1147.

December 10, 1948 (with **The X-Rays**)
    Willie Moore, Chippy Outcalt, George Rhodes, Walter Page,
    Bobby Donaldson, X-Rays, Milt Larkin (vocals)

    I'll Always Be in Love with You/Teddy's Dreams/Beef Stew/

One for Willie/Neck Bones

Second, fourth and fifth titles on SJL-1147; third title on SJL-2234.

February 9, 1949
Willie Moore, Chippy Outcalt, Tate Houston, Walter Buchanan, Butch Ballard

Happy Days

SJL-2234.

Billy Stewart/Milton Buggs (with Ray Abrams Orch.)
February 18, 1947
February 18, 1949

Charlie Ventura
August 28, 1945
Arnold Ross, John Levy, Specs Powell

Charlie Comes On/Big Deal/Ever So Thoughtful/Jackpot/Dark Eyes

All on Savoy MG12200, Charlie Kennedy & Charlie Ventura: *Crazy Rhythms*.

Kenny Watts
August 9, 1946

Paul Williams
September 5, 1947
John Lawton, Walter Cox, T. J. Fowler, Hank Ivory, Clarence Stamps, Alex Thomas

Hastings Street Bounce/Paradise Valley Walk/Way Late

October 6, 1947
as above

Bouncing with Benson/Come with Me Baby/3530

Last title on SJL-2221, *The Roots of Rock 'n' Roll.*

November 20, 1947

December 20, 1947

March 2, 1948
Phil Guilbeau, Wild Bill Moore, Floyd Taylor, Herman Hopkins, Reetham Mallett

Waxie Maxie/Spider Sent Me/The Twister, 1 & 2

Third title on SJL-2234, *The Roots of Rock 'n' Roll, v. 6.*

March 4, 1948
as on last session

Turtle Rock/Canadian Ace

Both on SJL-2234, *The Roots of Rock 'n' Roll, v. 6.*

December 15, 1948
Phil Guilbeau, Miller Sam, Floyd Taylor, Herman Hopkins, Reetham Mallett

Free Dice/The Hucklebuck

Last title on SJL-2221, *The Roots of Rock 'n' Roll* and Saxophonograph BP-500, *The Hucklebuck: Paul Williams and His Orchestra.*

January 13, 1949
James Poe, Billy Mitchell, Louis Barrett, Floyd Taylor, John Holiday, Bill Benjamin, Joan Shaw

Rompin'/Brown Derby Boogie/Popcorn/Barbecue/Jelly Roll Boogie/House Rocker/He Knows How to Hucklebuck/Back Bender

First, sixth, and seventh titles on SJL-2234, *The Roots of Rock 'n' Roll, v. 6.*

December 1, 1949

May 18, 1950

February 26, 1951

July 25, 1951

Rubberlegs Williams
April 24, 1945
> Miles Davis, Herbie Fields, Ted Brannon, Al Casey, Leonard Gaskin, Ed Nicholson
>
> That's the Stuff You Gotta Watch/Pointless Mama Blues/Deep Sea Blues/Bring It on Home
>
> All titles, with newly discovered alternates and fragments, on Savoy SJL-1196, Miles Davis: *First Miles.*

Kai Winding
December 14, 1945
> Shorty Rogers, Stan Getz, Shorty Allen, Iggy Shevack, Shelly Manne
>
> Sweet Miss/Loaded/Grab Your Axe, Max/Always
>
> Complete session, including alternates, on SJL-1105, Stan Getz: *Opus De Bop.*

Billy Wright
September 23, 1949

Lester Young
June 28, 1949
> Jesse Drakes, Jerry Elliott, Junior Mance, Leroy Jackson, Roy Haynes
>
> Crazy Over J.Z./Ding Dong/Blue 'n' Bells/June Bug
>
> All titles, including alternates, on SJL-2202, Lester Young: *Pres, The Complete Savoy Recordings.*

ROOST

Tony Aless
July 1955
Long Island Suite (LP-2202)

Reissued on Fresh Sounds RLP-2202.

Georgie Auld
January 24, 1951
Frank Rosolino, Lou Levy, Max Bennett, Tiny Kahn

Seh Seh/Be My Love (524)
New Airmail Special/Out of Nowhere (523)
Autumn in New York/You Made Me Love You (564)
Taps Miller/What's New? (527)
The Things We Did Last Summer (LP-403)

All except "Autumn" and "The Things" on Jazz American Marketing JAM-5006, *Unearthed Masters, v. 1: Parker/Hawkins/Auld.*

Harry Belafonte
1949
Orchestra including Howard McGhee, Brew Moore

Recognition/Lean on Me (501)

Eddie Bonnemere
The following sides were made at several sessions, ca. 1952-54:

There Goes My Heart/White Christmas (583)
Five O'Clock Whistle/Ti-Pi-Ti-Pi-Tin (585)
True/Square Dance Mambo (590)
Mambo in the Moonlight/Muskrat Ramble (597)
Oriental Mambo/El Ultimo (600)
Roostology/Trolley Song (602)
Charmaine/Golden Moon (607)

Bo Diddley/The Man in the Raincoat (608)
Cherry Meringue/Charleston Mambo (611)

1959
Piano Bon Bons (LP-2236*)

1960
The Sound of Memory (LP-2241*)

Eddie "Lockjaw" Davis
1952
  Bill Doggett, Oscar Pettiford, Shadow Wilson

  My Blue Heaven/Bewitched (553)
  Please Don't Talk about Me/Blues in My Heart (559)

December 1952
  Billy Taylor, Freddie Greene, Oscar Pettiford, Shadow Wilson

  There's No You/Hey Lock (565)
  Slow Squat/Old Cowhand (572)

  NOTE: First two titles listed in most discographies as issued on
  Roost 568, which is actually by Johnny Smith.

1952-53
  accompanied by Eddie Bonnemere

  This Can't Be Love/Bongo Domingo (601)

1953
Goodies (LP-422 [10"])

May 1958
Eddie Lockjaw Davis, Introducing Shirley Scott (LP-2227)

Stan Getz
May 17, 1950
  Al Haig, Tommy Potter, Roy Haynes

  Yesterdays/Sweetie Pie (512)
  Gone with the Wind/Hershey Bar (516)
  On the Alamo (522)
  You Go to My Head (578)

December 10, 1950
  Horace Silver, Joe Calloway, Walter Bolden

Tootsie Roll/Strike Up the Band (520)
Imagination (EP306)
For Stompers Only (522)
Navy Blue (LP-2258)
Out of Nowhere/'S Wonderful (596)

March 1, 1950
as above

Split Kick/The Best Thing for You (526)
It Might as Well Be Spring (550)
Penny (556)

August 15, 1951
Horace Silver, Jimmy Raney, Leonard Gaskin, Roy Haynes

Melody Express (570)
Yvette/Potter's Luck (538)
The Song Is You (550)
Wildwood (556)

NOTE: Most discographies list the bassist as Leonard Gaskin or
Tommy Potter; Gaskin has confirmed his presence.

October 1951
At Storyville, v. 2 (LP-2225*)

December 5, 1952
Duke Jordan, Jimmy Raney, Bill Crow, Frank Isola

Lullaby of Birdland/Autumn Leaves (562)
Fools Rush In (578)
These Foolish Things (570)

NOTE: Bassist Bill Crow recalls that this session actually took
place a week later, after Getz's first date for Norgran on December
12. Reig wanted all Roost artists to make a version of "Lullaby of
Birdland." Getz agreed, but since he was now under contract to
Norman Granz, the Roost session was assigned the earlier date.

NOTE: Some of the Getz Roost 78s also issued on *The Greatest of
Getz* (LP-2249*) [reissued as Roulette SR-59027], *The Getz Age*
(LP-2258*), and Jazz America Marketing JAM-5007, *The Un-
earthed Masters—v. 2: Stan Getz.*

Terry Gibbs
1964
El Latino! (LP-2260*)

Tyree Glenn
1951
  Bill Doggett, John Simmons, Jo Jones

  Tell Me Why/The Little White Cloud That Cried (543)
  Wrap Your Troubles in Dreams/Sugar (557)

1952
  Hank Jones, Milt Hinton, Jo Jones

  Sidewalks of New York/How Could You Do a Thing Like That
  To Me? (612)

Prince Happiness (*see* **King Pleasure**)

Johnny Hartman
1959
And I Thought About You (LP-2232*)

  Reissued on Fresh Sounds FSR-567.

Coleman Hawkins
August 25, 1950
  Billy Taylor, Percy Heath, Art Blakey

  Can Anyone Explain?/I Cross My Fingers (517)
  You Got Me Crying Again/I'll Know (519)

  "Can Anyone Explain?" and "You Got Me Crying" on Jazz
  America Marketing JAM-5006, *Unearthed Masters—v. 1: Parker/
  Hawkins/Auld.* All four titles on Swingtime 1004,
  Coleman Hawkins: *Hawk Variations.*

Beverley Kenney
1955
Sings for Johnny Smith (LP-2206)

Reissued on Fresh Sounds RLP-2206.

1956
With Jimmy Jones and the Basie-ites (LP-2218)

Reissued on Fresh Sounds FSR-614.

Mary Ann McCall
February 1, 1950

Red Rodney, Earl Swope, Al Cohn, Gerry Mulligan, Al Haig, Curly Russell, Jeff Morton

The Sky Is Crying/After I Say I'm Sorry (511)
I Cried for You/Until the Real Thing Comes Along (514)

Howard McGhee
1949?

Cubop City 1 & 2 (502)

Oscar Pettiford
October 1952
Billy Taylor, Charles Mingus, Charlie Smith

Cello Again/Sonny Boy (546)
Ah-Dee-Dong Blues/I'm Beginning to See the Light (561)

Alternates of all four masters issued on Savoy SJL-1172, Oscar Pettiford: *Discoveries.*

King Pleasure
1951-52

Lester Leaps In/All Alone and Blue (554)

NOTE: Issued under pseudonym Prince Happiness.

Bud Powell
January 10, 1947
Curly Russell, Max Roach

Somebody Loves Me/Bud's Bubble (509)

I'll Remember April/Off Minor (513)
Indiana/Everything Happens to Me (518)
I Should Care/Nice Work if You Can Get It (521)

All on Roost RLP-412, *The Bud Powell Trio* [reissued on Japanese Roulette SL-5044-RO].

NOTE: Session originally recorded for DeLuxe.

Seldon Powell
October/November 1955
Seldon Powell Plays (LP-2205)

1956
Sextet, Featuring Jimmy Cleveland (LP-2220)

Reissued on Fresh Sounds FSR-588.

Arsenio Rodriguez (*see* Latin section)

Little Jimmy Scott
1951-52

I Got It Bad/The Masquerade Is Over (530)
Don't Cry My Heart/Pretty Eyes (540)
My Mother's Eyes/Hands across the Table (536)
Be My Sunshine/I'll Understand (551)
Cherry/Cryin' My Heart Out for You (555)

March 20, 1952
Terry Gibbs, Howard Biggs, Hy White, Louis Bellson

I'll Close My Eyes/Why Do You Cry? (603)

Johnny Smith (*see also* Miscellaneous section for Verve productions)
March 11, 1952
Stan Getz, Sanford Gold, Eddie Safranski, Don Lamond

Where or When (558)
Moonlight in Vermont/Tabu (547)
Jaguar (568)

Complete session and many of the 78 sides from next sessions on LP-2211, Johnny Smith: *Moonlight in Vermont*; reissued as LP-2251, *Johnny Smith and Stan Getz* and Fresh Sounds RLP-410, *Moonlight in Vermont*.

April 1952
  Zoot Sims replaces Getz

  Ghost of a Chance (558)
  Villa (573)

November 1952
  Stan Getz, Sanford Gold, Bob Carter, Morey Feld

  Sometimes I'm Happy (579)
  Stars Fell on Alabama (573)
  Nice Work if You Can Get It (EP-310)
  Tenderly (568)

June 5, 1953
  Joe Mooney, Eddie Safranski, Don Lamond

  Ramona/Limelight (574)

June 6, 1953
  Zoot Sims, Sanford Gold, Eddie Safranski, Don Lamond

  My Funny Valentine (579)

July 1953
  Paul Quinichette, Sanford Gold, Arnold Fishkin, Don Lamond

  Cavu/I'll Be Around (581)

  NOTE: Many discographies erroneously list Zoot Sims instead of Quinichette for this session.

August 1953
  Paul Quinichette, Sanford Gold, Arnold Fishkin, Don Lamond

  Yesterdays/Cherokee (586)

1953
  Arnold Fishkin, Don Lamond

  Lullaby of Birdland/My One and Only Love (589)
  What's New?/I'll Remember April (593)

1954
  Perry Lopez, Arnold Fishkin, Don Lamond

Sophisticated Lady/Easy to Love (594)
Lover Man/Stranger in Paradise (598)
Our Love Is Here to Stay/'S Wonderful (LP-421)

1955
Moods, Moods, Moods (LP-2215)

September 1955
Johnny Smith Plays Jimmy Van Heusen (LP-2201)

Reissue: LP-2250*.

October 1955
Quartet (LP-2203)

September 1956
The New Johnny Smith Quartet (LP-2216)

Reissued on Fresh Sounds M-5159.

1956
Foursome (LP-2223)

Reissued on Fresh Sounds FSR-581.

September 1957
Foursome, v. 2 (LP-2228)

Reissued on Fresh Sounds SLP-2228.

January 1959
The Flower Drum Song (LP-2231*)

February 1959
Easy Listening (LP-2233*)

July 1959
Favorites (LP-2237*)

1959-60
Designed for You (LP-2238)

1960
My Dear Little Sweetheart (LP-2239*)

1960
Guitar and Strings (LP-2242*)

1960
Johnny Smith Plus the Trio (LP-2243*)

1961
The Sound of Johnny Smith's Guitar (LP-2246*)

Reissued on Fresh Sounds FSR-583.

1963-64
Reminiscing (LP-2259*)

Herbie Steward
January 17, 1949
Al Haig, Jimmy Raney, Curly Russell, Roy Haynes

Medicine Man/Passport to Pimlico (515) T'Ain't No Use/Sinbad the Sailor (510)

February 9, 1951
Dick Hyman, Mert Oliver, Don Lamond

This Is My Last Affair/My Baby Just Cares for Me (525)

Sonny Stitt
May 1952
Billy Taylor, John Simmons, Jo Jones

Why Do I Love You/Symphony Hall Swing (560)

May 1952
Johnny Richards Orchestra: Don Elliott, Kai Winding, Sid Cooper, George Berg, Horace Silver, Charles Mingus, Don Lamond

Sancho Panza/If I Could Be with You (571)
Hooke's Tours/Sweet and Lovely (576)

June 1952
as above, but Jerry Sanfino, Al Williams, and Jo Jones replace Cooper, Silver, and Lamond

Harvest Moon/Opus 202 (595)
Loose Talk/Pink Satin (LP-415)

1952
Dean Earl, Bernard Griggs, Marquis Foster

Every Tub/Blue and Sentimental/Pennies from Heaven/Thou Swell (LP-415)

1953
Battle of Birdland [with Eddie Lockjaw Davis] (LP-1203)

September/October 1955
Sonny Stitt: Arrangements by Quincy Jones (LP-2204)

September 1956
Sonny Stitt Plays (LP-2208)

1956
37 Minutes and 48 Seconds (LP-2219)

June 1957
Sonny Stitt with the New Yorkers (LP-2226)

 Reissued on Fresh Sounds FSR-570.

January 1959
The Saxophones of Sonny Stitt (LP-2230*)

June 1959
A Little Bit of Stitt (LP-2235)

March 1960
The Sonny Side of Stitt (LP-2240)

1960
Stittsville (LP-2244)

1960
Sonny Side Up (LP-2245*)

1961-62
Feelin's . . . (LP-2247*)

1963
Stitt in Orbit (LP-2252)

1963
Stitt Goes Latin (LP-2253)

1965
Sax Expressions (LP-2262*)

Billy Taylor (pianist)
November 1, 1951
 Mundell Lowe, Earl May, Jo Jones, Zoot Sims, Frank Conlon

 Cu-Blue/Squeeze Me (537)
 Cuban Caper/Feeling Frisky (566)

May 2, 1952
> Chuck Wayne, Earl May, Charlie Smith, Frank Conlon, Manny Quendo
>
> Cuban Nightingale/Makin' Whoopee (552)
> Titoro/Moonlight Savings Time (LP-409)

Kai Winding
April 1949
> Brew Moore, Gerry Mulligan, George Wallington, Curly Russell, Max Roach
>
> Bop City/Wallington's Godchild (500)
> Crossing the Channel/Sleepy Bop (503)
>
> All on Roost 408 (10" LP).

May 31, 1951
> Brew Moore, Lou Stein, Jack Lesberg, Don Lamond
>
> Honey/Someone to Watch over Me/Cheek to Cheek/Harlem Buffet
>
> All on Roost 401 (10" LP).

ROULETTE

Pearl Bailey
1958
Naughty but Nice (R-25125*)

1958-59
More Songs for Adults Only (R-25101*)

1959
Songs of the Bad Old Days (R-25116*)

1961
The Best of Pearl Bailey (R-25144*)

   Reissued on CD: Roulette RCD-59050.

January 1962
Happy Sounds (R-25167*)

   NOTE: With Louie Bellson.

Louie Bellson
1961
Around the World in Percussion (R-65002*)

January 1962
Big Band Jazz from the Summit (R-52087*)

   Reissued on Fresh Sounds R-52087.

Louie Bellson/Gene Krupa
1963
The Mighty Two (R-52089*)

Louie Bellson/Lalo Schifrin
1962
Explorations (R-52120)

166

Willie Bobo (*see* Latin section)

Sharkey Bonano
January 1960
Dixieland at the Roundtable (R-25112*)

Candido (*see* Latin section)

Eddie "Lockjaw" Davis
March 1958
Eddie Davis Trio (R-52019*)

Cora Lee Day
1960
My Crying Hour (R-52048*)

Billy Eckstine
1960
Once More With Feeling (R-25104*)

1960
No Cover, No Minimum (R-52052*)

Harry Edison
November 1958
Sweetenings (R-52023*)

February 1960
Patented by Edison (R-52041*)

Maynard Ferguson
June 1959
Message from Birdland (R-52027*)

October 1959
Plays Music for Dancing (R-52038*)

March 1960
Newport Suite (R-52047*)

1960
Maynard '61 (R-52064*)

Reissued on Fresh Sounds R-52064.

1962
Maynard '62 (R-52083*)

1962
Si! Si!—M.F. (R-52084*)

Reissued on Fresh Sounds R-52084.

1963
Maynard '63 (R-52090*)

Maynard Ferguson/Chris Connor
1961
Two's Company (R-52068*)

Reissued on Fresh Sounds R-52068.

Tyree Glenn
1959
Try a Little Tenderness (R-25075)

John Handy III
1959
In the Vernacular (R-52042*)

1961
No Coast Jazz (R-52058*)

1962
Jazz: John Handy III (R-52121*)

Illinois Jacquet
1958-59
Illinois Jacquet Flies Again (R-53035*)

Ella and Buddy Johnson
December 1958
Go Ahead and Rock (R-25085*)

Machito (*see* Latin section)

Mitchell-Ruff Duo (Dwike Mitchell, Willie Ruff)
May 1958
Mitchell-Ruff Duo + Strings and Brass (R-52013*)

1960
The Sound of Music (R-52037*)

Turk Murphy
April 1959
Turk Murphy and His Jazz Band at the Roundtable (R-25076*)

April 1959
Music for Wise Guys, Etc. (R-25088*)

Phineas Newborn
June 1959
Piano Portraits (R-52031*)

October 1959
I Love a Piano (R-52043*)

Joe Newman
May 1958
Joe Newman With Woodwinds (R-52014*)

Tito Puente (*see* Latin section)

Don Redman
March 1959
Dixieland in High Society (R-25070*)

Salt City Six
1959-60
Dixieland at the Roundtable (R-25080*)

Jeri Southern/Johnny Smith
1958
Jeri Southern Meets Johnny Smith (R-25016*)

   Reissued on Fresh Sounds R-52016.

Jack Teagarden
July 1959
Jack Teagarden at the Roundtable (R-25091*)

January 1960
Jazz Maverick (R-25119*)

1961
A Portrait of Mr. T. (R-25243*)

Sarah Vaughan
April 1960
Dreamy (R-52046*) [arr. & cond. by Jimmy Jones]

   Reissued on Fresh Sounds SR-52046.

1961
The Divine One (R-52060)

June 1961
After Hours (R-52070)

1962
You're Mine, You (R-52082*) [arr. & cond. by Quincy Jones]

1962
Snowbound (R-52091*)

1962
The Explosive Side of Sarah Vaughan (R-52092*) [arr. & cond. by
   Benny Carter]

1962-63
Star Eyes (R-52100*)

January 1963
The Lonely Hours (R-52104*) [arr. by Benny Carter]

1964
Sarah Sings Soulfully (R-52116*) [arr. & cond. by Gerald Wilson]

1964
Sarah + 2 (R-52118*)

Reissued on Fresh Sounds FSR-605.

Randy Weston
November/December 1960
Uhuru Afrika (Freedom Africa) (R-65001*) [Weston: music; Langston
  Hughes: lyrics]

Joe Williams
October 1957
A Man Ain't Supposed to Cry (R-52005*)

  NOTE: Produced with Hugo and Luigi.
  Reissued on CD: Roulette RCD-59023.

July 1959
Joe Williams Sings about You (R-52030*)

1959
That Kind of Woman (R-52039*)

1959
One Is a Lonesome Number (R-52102*)

1960
Sentimental and Melancholy (R-52066*)

1961
Have a Good Time with Joe Williams (R-52071*) [with Harry Edison
  & His Orchestra]

Joe Williams/Harry Edison
February 1961
Together (Roulette R-52069*)

  Reissued on Fresh Sounds FSR-603.

Bob Wyatt
1958-59
The Happy Organ of Bob Wyatt (R25087*)

COUNT BASIE (all labels)

October 1957
Basie (E = mc²) (Roulette R-52003*)

> NOTE: This is known as the "Atomic Bomb" album. Reissued as Roulette SR-59025/CD: RCD-59025.

December 1957
Count Basie Presents the Eddie Davis Trio + Joe Newman (Roulette R-52007*)

April 1958
Basie Plays Hefti (Roulette R-52011*)

April 1958
Chairman of the Board (Roulette R-52032*)

May/September/October 1958
Sing Along with Basie (Roulette R-52018*)

> NOTE: With Lambert, Hendricks & Ross, Joe Williams. Reissued on CD: Roulette RCD-59041.

September/October 1958/September 1959/September 1960
Back to Basie and the Blues (Roulette R-52093*)

> NOTE: With Joe Williams.

October/December 1958
Memories Ad Lib (Roulette R-52021*)

> NOTE: With Joe Williams.

Reissued on CD: Roulette RCD-59037.

December 1958/January 1959
One More Time (Roulette R-52024*)

NOTE: From the pen of Quincy Jones.
Produced with Rudy Traylor.

January 1959
Count Basie Swings—Tony Bennett Sings (Roulette R-25072*)

Reissued as R-25231, *Strike Up the Band* [CD: RCD-59021].

May 1959
Breakfast Dance and Barbecue (Roulette R-52028*)

NOTE: With Joe Williams.

May/June 1959
Basie/Eckstine/Incorporated (Roulette R-52029*)

Reissued on CD: Roulette RCD-59042.

September 1957/September 1958/September 1959
Everyday I Have the Blues (Roulette R-52033*)

NOTE: With Joe Williams.

December 1959
Dance Along with Basie (Roulette R-52036*)

June 1959/May 1960
String Along with Basie (Roulette R-52051*)

June 1960
Not Now, I'll Tell You When (Roulette R-52044*)

June 1960
The Best of Basie (Roulette R-52081*)

Reissued on CD: Roulette RCD-59035.

June 1960
The Best of Basie, vol. 2 (Roulette R-52089*)

Reissued on CD: Roulette RCD-58036.

September 1960
Just the Blues (Roulette R-52054*)

NOTE: With Joe Williams.

September 1960
Kansas City Suite: The Music of Benny Carter (Roulette R-52056*)

January/March 1961
Count Basie/Sarah Vaughan (Roulette R-52061*)

Reissued on CD: Roulette RCD-59043.

June 1961
Basie at Birdland (Roulette R-52065)

Reissued on CD: Roulette RCD-59039.

October/November 1961
The Legend (Roulette R-52086*)

NOTE: From the pen of Benny Carter.
Reissued on CD: Roulette RCD-59038.

July 1962
Easin' It (Roulette R-52106*)

July 1962
Back with Basie (Roulette R-52113*)

August 1962
Basie in Sweden (Roulette R-52099*)
Reissued on CD: Roulette RCD-59040.

April 1963
Li'l Ol' Groovemaker (Verve V6-8549)

December 1964
Pop Goes the Basie (Reprise R-6153*)

January 1965
Basie Picks the Winners (Verve V6-8616*)

October 1965/February 1967
Basie's Beat (Verve V6-8687*)

December 1965
Arthur Prysock/Count Basie (Verve V6-8646)
   NOTE: Produced by Creed Taylor. Reig credited: "Basie band under the supervision of Teddy Reig."

December 1965
Basie Meets Bond (United Artists UA-3480/UAS-6480*)

May 1966
Basie's Beatle Bag (Verve V6-8659*)
   NOTE: Produced with Peter Spargo.

June 1966
Basie Swingin', Voices Singin' (ABC-Paramount 570*)
NOTE: Produced with Bob Thiele.

August/September 1966
Broadway, Basie's Way (Command RS-905SD*)
NOTE: Produced with Loren Becker and Robert Byrne.

December 1966/January 1967
Hollywood, Basie's Way (Command RS-912SD*)
NOTE: Produced with Loren Becker and Robert Byrne.

August 1967
Basie's in the Bag (Brunswick BL-54127*)

October 1967
The Happiest Millionaire (Coliseum D-41003/DS-51003*)
NOTE: Production credited to "Teddy Riggs."

November 1967
Half a Sixpence (Dot DLP-3834/DLP-25834*)
NOTE: Produced with Tom Mack.

November 1967
Count Basie & the Mills Brothers (Dot DLP-3838/DLP-25838)

January 1968
Jackie Wilson/Count Basie: Manufacturers of Soul (Brunswick BL-54134/BL-754134*)
NOTE: Produced with Nat Tarnopol. Liner notes by Teddy Reig.

July 1968
Count Basie & the Mills Brothers: The Board of Directors (Dot DLP-3888/25838*)

NOTE: Produced with Tom Mack.

September 1968
Basie Straight Ahead (Dot DLP-25902*)

NOTE: Produced with Tom Mack.

December 1968
Kay Starr/Count Basie (Gold Star 150.0006*)

NOTE: Produced with Dick Pierce and Tom Mack.

January 1969
Standing Ovation (Dot DLP-25938*)

NOTE: Produced with Tom Mack. Reissued on ABC AC-30004, *Count Basie Orchestra: The ABC Collection.*

October 1969/February 1970
Basic Basie (BASF MC-25111) (2-record set)

NOTE: "A & R supervision: Teddy Reig."
Reissue: Verve MPS 821291-1/821291-2. CD: MPS 82191-2.

LATIN (all labels)

Willie Bobo
1963
El Watusi (Roulette 66-69 [45 rpm single])

1963
Bobo's Beat (Roulette R-52097)

1963?
Bobo! Do That Thing (Tico LP-1108*)

1964
Let's Go Bobo (Roulette R-25272*)

September 1966
Feelin' So Good (Verve V6-8669*)

    NOTE: Produced with Pete Spargo.

January/February 1967
Juicy (Verve V6-8685*)

    NOTE: Produced with Pete Spargo.

July 1967
Bobo Motion (Verve V6-8699*)

    NOTE: Produced with Pete Spargo.

February 1968
Spanish Blues Band (Verve V6-8736*)

    NOTE: Produced with Pete Spargo.

Candido
1962
Conga Soul (Roulette R-52078*)

Santos Colon
Stop and Listen! (Tico LP-1147)

Joe Cuba
Canciones Mi Mama (Tico LP-1111)

Hangin' Out (Tico LP-1112)

Alma Del Barrio (Tico LP-1119)

Mas Canciones Mi Mama (Tico LP-1120)

Bailadores (Tico LP-1124)

Jorge Dalto
1976
Chevere (United Artists LA-671*)

    NOTE: This was Teddy Reig's last production.

Graciela
Esta Es Graciela (Tico LP-1107*)

    NOTE: With Machito.

Intimo y Sentimental (Tico LP-1123)

    NOTE: With Machito.

Pupi Legarreta
Salsa Nova (Tico LP-1091*)

Machito
1958
With Flute to Boot (Roulette R-52026*)

Chico O'Farrill
September 1967
Married Well (Verve V6-5035)

    NOTE: Produced with Pete Spargo.

Eddie Palmieri
Azucar (Tico LP-1122)

Mambo Con Conga Is Mozambique (Tico LP-1126*)

Molasses (Tico LP-1148)

Bamboleate (Tico LP-1150)

Patato and Totico [Carlos (Patato) Valdes/Totico (Juan Drake)]
September 1967
Patato y Totico (Verve V6-5037)

Tito Puente
1964
My Fair Lady Goes Latin (Roulette R-25276)

World (Tico LP-1109)

Mucho Puente (Tico LP-1115)

Tito Puente/Lupe
late 1964
Tito Puente Swings—Exciting Lupe Sings (Tico LP-1121)

Arsenio Rodriguez
Pachango (Tico LP-1092)

1965
Primitivo (Roost LP-2261)

Lalo Schifrin
Piano Espanol (Tico LP-1070)

Miguelito Valdes
Reunion (Tico LP-1098)

Mexico Yo Te Canto (Tico LP-1110)

September 1967
Inolvidables (Verve V6-5036)

   NOTE: Produced with Pete Spargo.

MISCELLANEOUS

Belle Barth
date?
In Person (Laughtime LT-901*)

Zoot Sims
October 1956
Zoot (Argo 608)

> NOTE: Reig has indicated that he produced this session. The original issue does not list a producer, although the reissue (under the same catalog number) states: "Album production—Dave Usher."

Johnny Smith (*see also* Roost section)
March 1967
Johnny Smith (Verve V6-8692*)

November 1967
Johnny Smith's Kaleidoscope (Verve V6-8737*)

November 1968
Phase II (Verve V6-8767*)

NOTES

1. The arrests and trial received extensive coverage in the *New York Times*: January 1, 1943, p. 25; January 9, 1943, p. 11; January 23, 1943, p. 28; January 24, 1943, p. 44; February 23, 1943, p. 24; February 25, 1943, p. 26; February 26, 1943, p. 21; February 27, 1943, p.15; February 28, 1943, p. 43; March 31, 1943, p. 21; April 28, 1943, p. 25. *Down Beat* ran a synopsis of the affair under the front-page headline, "Tea Scandal Stirs Musicdom" (January 15, 1943).

    This very complicated chain of events began with the friendship between Mike Bryan, who was in the army at the time, and novelist Ursula Parrott. It not only resulted in drug charges against Bryan, Reig and Georgie Auld (also in the service), but a court-martial against Bryan for desertion. The precise chronology is not clear from the press reports, but apparently some time in December of 1942, Parrott enticed Bryan to accompany her to New York from Miami where he was stationed. She then used him to obtain evidence for a prosecutor from the Federal Bureau of Narcotics, exposing an alleged "ring" supplying marijuana to servicemen. Despite allusions to a "reefer parlor" and the widespread involvement of servicemen, the evidence cited does not seem to implicate anyone other than the immediate participants: Reig, Bryan, Auld, and singer Rose Reynolds. The *Down Beat* article takes pains to point out that Reig's participation came about only as a favor to his friends. Reig was described as "a mutual friend who had been around the business for years and knew everyone connected with it." *Down Beat* further notes that "Reig made no profit, [he was] merely obliging Miss Reynolds and Bryan." The article reports that Reig went uptown to make the purchase from a friend of his named "Pork Chops," and shortly thereafter, made another purchase, at Bryan's request, "from a character named Zombi." The press referred to Reig as a "nightclub master of ceremonies" and asserted that he often went under the name of "Teddy Reede."

    At one point in this bizarre episode, Parrott assisted Bryan in escaping from a Miami Beach stockade, where he was held for having gone AWOL. Parrott was indicted for harboring a deserter and impairing the discipline and morale of the armed forces. In April 1943, Reig was sentenced to a year and a day. Bryan and Auld received suspended sentences, and Parrott was acquitted.

2. March 13, 1944, reissued on Savoy SJL-2216, *All Star Swing Groups.*

3. In the interviews, Reig alludes to having produced a Joe Venuti date for Decca, even before the Continental session: "When I was just starting out in the business, I recorded Joe Venuti over at Decca. There were four boxes for the four tunes, and I was supposed to supply all the label information on each. After they cut the first one, I asked Joe for the title and he said, 'A little later.' By the time they finished the second tune I still had nothing on paper and was afraid the boss might come in. So I said, 'Please Mr. Venuti. I need the titles.' He said, 'Come here. The first tune is "Something." The second tune is "Nothing." The third tune is "Flip," and the fourth is "Flop." You got it? Now stop bothering me!'" Given the fact that these Venuti sides were made on January 25, 1939, it is highly unlikely that Reig, who was twenty years old, could have "produced" them. It is possible that he was hired in a lesser capacity (which involved logging the performances), or was simply present on an informal basis.

4. The Don Byas "Laura" session took place on September 6, 1945; there is no corresponding Savoy session listed in Ruppli for that date.

5. Much of the section on Parker comes from Bob Porter's 1978 interview with Teddy which was included in the booklet to Savoy SJL-5500, Charlie Parker: *The Complete Savoy Studio Sessions.* This material is used with the permission of Bob Porter.

6. Aural evidence indicates the presence of another pianist, probably Hakim. See notes by James Patrick, ibid.

7. April 18, 1944 (Earle Warren and His Orchestra) and May 1, 1944. Reissued on Savoy SJL-2202, Lester Young: *Pres—The Complete Savoy Recordings.*

8. Williams remembers this rehearsal as having taken place at the Royal Theater in Baltimore (see Paul Williams interview).

9. March 22, 1949, Victor 20-3427; reissued on LP, RCA ANL1-2162, Tommy Dorsey: *On the Sunny Side.*

10. June 23, 1949, Harmony 1049; reissued on LP, Foxy 9007/8, *Oran "Hot Lips" Page, v. 2.*

11. April 10, 1949, Columbia 38486; reissued on LP, Columbia CL-2741, *The Essential Sinatra, v. 3.*
12. May 1946, Haven 800.
13. October 1957, Roulette R-52003, *Basie (E = mc²).*
14. Ibid.
15. Ibid.
16. January 1969, Dot DLP-25938, *Standing Ovation.*
17. Buena Vista 3308.
18. July 6, 1961, Columbia CS-8515; reissue: Columbia CJ-40586.
19. December 22, 1958, Columbia CS-8104, *In Person!*
20. Roulette R-52060, *The Divine One.*
21. Probably Tico 1092, *Pachanga.*
22. Tico 1122.
23. Tico 1121, *Tito Puente Swings—Exciting Lupe Sings.*
24. See interview with Peter Spargo.
25. Verve V6-5037, *Patato y Totico*, Carlos (Patato) Valdes and Totico (Juan Drake).
26. June 1975, Pablo 2310-771, *Afro-Cuban Jazz Moods.*
27. This album, Teddy Reig's last production, is United Artists LA-671, *Chevere*, by Jorge Dalto.
28. February 25, 1946, for Savoy.
29. May 2, 1945, for Duke.
30. September 8, 1949, 3 Deuces label.
31. Abbey 15003.
32. For extensive interviews with Wexler, see Timothy White, "Jerry Wexler: The Godfather of Rhythm & Blues," *Rolling Stone*, November 27, 1980, and Ted Fox, *In the Groove* (listed in Bibliography).
33. September 5, 1947.
34. October 6, 1947.
35. Reig recorded Leo Parker in Detroit on October 4, 1947, just two days before Paul Williams' second session.
36. December 15, 1948.
37. For futher information, see Robert Yelin, "Johnny Smith," *Guitar Player*, January 1982, p. 38.
38. 1953, *Jazz Studio*, Decca 8058.
39. Smith's version of "Walk, Don't Run" was recorded in 1960 on Roost LP-2243, *Johnny Smith Plus the Trio*; Atkins' recording is on RCA 6079, *Now and Then*; The Ventures' version is on Liberty LTAO-8053, *Golden Greats by the Ventures* and on CD: Blue Jay BJ-8818, *The Ventures.*
40. September 1967, Verve V6-5037, *Patato y Totico.*

41. September 1966, Verve V6-8659.
42. July 1967, Verve V6-8699.
43. May 1966, Verve V6-8659.
44. December 1965, Verve V6-8646.
45. The album credits state: "Basie band under the supervision of Teddy Reig."
46. August 1967, Brunswick BL-54127; liner notes by Stanley Dance.

BIBLIOGRAPHY

THE FOLLOWING WORKS were essential aids in compiling the discography:

Jorgen Grunnet Jepsen, *Jazz Records 1942-*. Holte, Denmark: Karl Emil Knudsen, 1963-1970.

Michel Ruppli, with Bob Porter, *The Savoy Label: A Discography*. Westport, Connecticut: Greenwood, 1980.

Michel Ruppli, with Bob Porter, *The Clef/Verve Labels: A Discography. Vol. II: The MGM Era*. Westport, Connecticut: Greenwood, 1986.

Chris Sheridan, *Count Basie: A Biodiscography*. Westport, Connecticut: Greenwood, 1986.

Other useful sources of background information include these works:

Chuck Berry, *The Autobiography*. New York: Harmony, 1987.

James M. Doran, *Erroll Garner: The Most Happy Piano*. Metuchen, New Jersey: Scarecrow Press and the Institute of Jazz Studies, 1985. [Interview with Teddy Reig, pp. 55-56]

Leonard Feather, "Coral's Girth of the Blues Is Dun & Bradstreet of Harlem," *Down Beat* (July 2, 1952), p. 6.

Ted Fox, *In the Groove: The People behind the Music*. New York: St. Martin's, 1986.

Dizzy Gillespie, with Al Fraser, *To Be or Not to Bop*. New York: Doubleday, 1979. [Interview with Teddy Reig, pp. 298-301]

Peter Grendysa, liner notes to *The Hucklebuck: Paul Williams and His Orchestra*. Saxophonograph BP-500, 1981.

James Patrick and Bob Porter, booklet accompanying box set, *Charlie Parker: The Complete Savoy Studio Sessions.* Savoy SJL-5500, 1978.

Arnold Shaw, *Honkers and Shouters: The Golden Years of Rhythm and Blues.* New York: Collier, 1978.

INDEX

This index includes all personal names, song and album titles, as well as selected venues mentioned in the text. Song titles are in quotation marks; album titles are in italics. Letters (A-P) refer to the sixteen-page photo insert.